Cambridge Elements ≡

Elements in Publishing and Book Culture
edited by
Samantha Rayner
University College London
Leah Tether
University of Bristol

AUTHORSHIP AND PUBLISHING
IN THE HUMANITIES

Marcel Knöchelmann
Yale University

CAMBRIDGE
UNIVERSITY PRESS

CAMBRIDGE
UNIVERSITY PRESS

Shaftesbury Road, Cambridge CB2 8EA, United Kingdom

One Liberty Plaza, 20th Floor, New York, NY 10006, USA

477 Williamstown Road, Port Melbourne, VIC 3207, Australia

314–321, 3rd Floor, Plot 3, Splendor Forum, Jasola District Centre,
New Delhi – 110025, India

103 Penang Road, #05–06/07, Visioncrest Commercial, Singapore 238467

Cambridge University Press is part of Cambridge University Press & Assessment,
a department of the University of Cambridge.

We share the University's mission to contribute to society through the pursuit of
education, learning and research at the highest international levels of excellence.

www.cambridge.org
Information on this title: www.cambridge.org/9781009223096

DOI: 10.1017/9781009223089

© Marcel Knöchelmann 2023

First published 2023

A catalogue record for this publication is available from the British Library.

ISBN 978-1-009-22309-6 Paperback
ISSN 2514-8524 (online)
ISSN 2514-8516 (print)

Authorship and Publishing in the Humanities

Elements in Publishing and Book Culture

DOI: 10.1017/9781009223089

First published online: July 2023

Marcel Knöchelmann

Yale University

Author for correspondence: Marcel Knöchelmann, marcel.knoechelmann@yale.edu

ABSTRACT: What is the point of publishing in the humanities? This Element provides an answer to this question. It builds on a unique set of quantitative and qualitative data to understand why humanities scholars publish. It looks at both basic characteristics such as publication numbers, formats, and perceptions, and differences of national academic settings alongside the influences of the UK's Research Excellence Framework and the German *Exzellenzinitiative*. The data involve a survey of more than 1,000 humanities scholars and social scientists in the UK and Germany, allowing for a comprehensive comparative study and a series of qualitative interviews. The resulting critique provides scholars and policymakers with an accessible and critical work about the particularities of authorship and publishing in the humanities. It also gives an account of the problems and struggles of humanities scholars in contributing to discourse and being recognised for their intellectual work.

KEYWORDS: publish or perish, Research Excellence Framework, *Exzellenzinitiative*, authorship and publishing, humanities

ISBNs: 9781009223096 (PB), 9781009223089 (OC)

ISSNs: 2514-8524 (online), 2514-8516 (print)

Contents

> The work is the death mask of its conception.
>
> ——WALTER BENJAMIN

1 Understanding Authorship and Publishing

What exactly is the point of publishing? The humanities form a cluster of disciplines – a branch of learning – that fosters understanding of what it means to be human.[1] Humanities scholars consider writing and the careful, qualitative engagement with text to be of utmost importance. Being a scholar means being in dialogue with others by engaging with the complexity of their thought and offering accounts of understanding. Publishing, one may assume, facilitates this dialogue. To publish does not mean to put information out there; to publish means to enter a discourse community with the motivation to participate and learn, to argue, disagree, and build upon disagreement. Publishing is as much about readership as it is about authorship; author and reader merge in the recursive structure of dialogue. Publishing, in this sense, is borne by the motivation to contribute to discourse and to keep the dialogue about understanding what it means to be human alive. This is one answer to the question of what the point of publishing is.

This book gives a different answer. It claims that the point of publishing is not to be a voice in a dialogue but to yield formal authorship. This answer accounts for the ways authorship fares as a shortcut for productivity, and how this shortcut impacts the dissemination of scholarship in the humanities. Underlying this is a subtle shift of the means and ends of publishing. Publishing could be thought of as in the outline above. The motivation to publish is bound to the end of contributing to discourse; it grows out of dialogue and the intention to be a voice in it. Recognition of the work of

---

[1] This ideal of scholarship in the humanities is both polarising and unifying. It is the indelible origin of humanities scholarship to be concerned with the *Menschengeschlecht* (German: humankind) (Dilthey, [1910] 1970: 89). See also newer outlines of it, such as Habermas (1971: 140–86), Garland (2012: 301), and Thomä (2019: 101).

a scholar is equally bound to this. There is no shortcut for this recognition; it requires engagement with dialogue. Authorship may fare as a reference, but it cannot assume the point of recognition itself. Readers might vouch for the quality of a voice, but only in the specific context of its engagement. This is an ideal of authorship that has probably never been fully realised.

At the opposite of such an ideal, authorship fares not as a reference but as the actual point of recognition. The formal reference of authorship translates to an assumed productivity. Many such formal references – for instance, accumulated on a curriculum vitae – mean that the scholar is highly productive. Scholars are seen to be leaders in their areas if these formalities account for specific publishing brands. They are likely to be skilled if their authorship references point to a wide range of specialist areas. In an academic setting that favours marketable output, such a list of formal authorship references is worth more than anything. Scholars who have such a list are visible and productive, and the institutions they work at can benefit from this visibility and productivity. It is not the scholarship but the fact of it being out there and the way it is externalised that count. Publishing becomes a means to showcase visibility and productivity. The motivation to publish is bound to this end; dialogue and the intention to be a voice in it become secondary.

This shift of means and ends is visible in the publishing practices of scholars today. Of course, by claiming that authorship is a shortcut for productivity, I do not claim that – along this gamut of means and ends – we have reached the extreme point where publishing is *only* a means to showcase visibility and productivity. The individual scholar in the humanities is still motivated by the desire to know, to contribute original accounts of understanding to an ongoing dialogue, and to engage with the complexity of the thought of others. No publication is empty. Thinking and writing precede publishing, and each publication is likely to find at least some kind of readership. It might receive a few citations even, which allows us to assume that it is included in some kind of dialogue. Each text exists in a tradition and is likely to feed into the discourse of teaching.

And yet, by claiming that authorship is a shortcut for productivity, I *do* wish to highlight that we have reached the extreme where publishing is *dominantly* a means to showcase visibility and productivity. This domination is the result of a governance of scholarship that wishes to market the modern university as a site of the production of world-leading output. This site needs to be efficiently managed; there are simply too many applications to sort through, grants to apply for, review deadlines to meet, and opportunities to make scholarly merit visible. As a research manager – or a scholar involved in the organisation of more than their own scholarly endeavours – it seems only intuitive to claim that efficiency is a necessity. It might be lamented: how else can scholars respond to the masses of publications, applications, and reviews? One may say: information is everywhere, and you need to rationalise it in order to master it. However, this intuition seems to counter the basic tenets of the humanities. Their principles of hermeneutics and historicity posit that subjective, qualitative engagement is required to make a qualitative judgement.

Surely, I can ask others to make a judgement for me; we might call it peer review. A publication's formal mark of having been judged – peer reviewed – allows for efficient measurement of a kind. But it precedes dialogue. It is a judgement that contributes to the formality of authorship without being able to tell us something about the afterlife of the work *in* dialogue. This afterlife cannot be efficiently measured, and more and more publications exacerbate this difficulty. Masses of publications disguise the individual contribution, and they require self-referential work in terms of initial, formal statements of judgement. This need to handle masses of publications – the mass of publications itself – is a symptom of the problem, rather than part of a solution. This efficiency based on formal authorship manifests quite particular terms of a competition.

Competition, Growth, and Efficiency

These terms can hardly take account of the subtler manifestations of scholarship. The chaos and complexity of notes, of teaching, of conceptional text, of elusive dialogues are hard to assess efficiently. Unpublished manuscripts require reading. Teaching is difficult to objectify, even by means of standardised evaluations. Does the best teacher performance really yield the best – the most educative, scholarly profitable, or culturally desirable – education? What is the value of critical, engaging teaching if the marketable names of institution – enhanced by Research Excellence Framework (REF) ratings and one-dimensional rankings – overshadow all else?

In the pursuit to be determined the most productive scholar – productive in terms of both innovation and output of ideas and truths – competition is crowded and fierce such that heuristic efficiency is required. The merito-cratic notion of widening participation – which claims that anyone is allowed to compete so long as they perform well in the terms prescribed – further increases competition, which again enforces the requirement of efficiency.

These mutually reinforcing mechanisms of competition and efficient management have reached an extreme in the sense of a self-referential *growth/trust spiral*. As there are more and more aspiring scholars, dis-courses get more crowded. Competitive funding regimes and career developments based on quantities of output further incentivise increasing numbers of publications. For instance, across epistemic genres, 'the output of philosophical publications has by far surpassed the increase of members of the profession' (Rescher, 2019: 750; translation by the author). Even in the smallest definition of one's philosophical area, there are too many new publications today (Marquard, 2020b). In this, 'academic philosophy shares with other disciplines ... the huge increase in the number of submissions to journals in the past few decades' (Crane, 2018: n.p.). Schneijderberg et al. (2022: 21) identify 'a crowding-out effect of tradi-tional publication cultures by a publication culture valorized in natural sciences', with fewer books and ever more articles, especially in the English language, being published in Germany. This overproduction pertains to journals more than to monographs, but the problem continues into the long form. That said, the *monograph crisis* is not a crisis in terms of materiality. The monograph is still highly valued. Nevertheless, 'more titles are published [in the arts and humanities in the UK] than even the most assiduous scholar could hope to read' (Jubb, 2017: 5). This is a crisis in terms of a mismatch of supply and demand, as the development of numbers shows (Thompson, 2005: 93–8). Monographs have become so differentiated that each copy is of interest to only a few hundred scholars, if at all. As a result of this overproduction, scholars seem to have less and less time to read in depth (Baveye, 2014).

This turns into a need for trusted sources. Scholars – conducting all sorts of evaluations of publications, promotions, and grants – hardly find the time to engage qualitatively in dialogue with the scholarship in evaluation. They require heuristics instead: output timelines, topic scopes, publishing brands, co-authorships, editorship, and so on; all those instances of information that make the formality of authorship start mattering more and more. Their defining characteristics become more differentiated and, again, more crowded, which sets forth another layer of growth.

The law of motion is that growth of output allows for growth of publishing venues that then requires enforced stratification of these venues. In turn, scholars can rely on a trusted set of formal characteristics for their daily scholarship and evaluation practices. This stratification enforces mechanisms of visibility and mass publication that trigger further demand to publish: to stay visible and to signpost productivity in the different formal dimensions.

The REF only reinforces this spiral, albeit its formally benign outline. The REF *could* be seen as a mechanism that inhibits crude growth; after all, it claims to value quality above quantity. It is also said to perform on peer review, and the qualitative assessment of peers might be seen as an original scholarly activity. In all these respects, we might assume that the REF works against such a spiral and the excess of external research management. The reality paints a different picture, however. It is best summarised by the following formula: the REF does not review past discourse as it was shaped from within; rather, discourse is shaped from without to be reviewed by a future REF.

The REF is the epitome of using communication to measure and market productivity. Publications – the original means enabling discourse – become means enabling authorship. The REF thus reinforces governance of competition for a type of output that increasingly affects not only aspiring – young – scholars but individuals across career levels in the UK. A scholar has to be *REFable* – indicating to departmental management their value to the department's future outcome in the REF. The REF does not even reward or interact with the individual scholar; they have to contribute their work to the productivity of the institution. They become replaceable since it is their output – a commodity in a market of exchangeable ideas – that counts, not the specificity of their thought, their engagement with dialogue, or the students this dialogue attracts. Such specificity is reserved to an elite at a few elite institutions. For them, it is a competition of qualitative differentiation, of developing a strong intellectual programme that serves as a foundation for future monographs or smaller output. Great performance in the REF seems predictable for these happy few. The rest – the large majority – have to compete in terms of unspecific scholarship. They have to gain the credit of *REFability* not for the REF itself but because the institutions require the REF's material and symbolic reward to attract further staff and students. The REF thrives on rated output, not on ideas.

This makes REFability a function of the dubious sphere of the *job market*. This job market is the everyday idiom of the struggle for recognition that works in terms of formal requirements. It suggests that the most valuable is the scholar that is the most productive in terms of formal output; you have to produce new output to become REFable.

Publish or Perish

A prominent name for the experienced pressure that this struggle exerts is *publish or perish*. It claims that either you publish or you perish. You may not clinically pass away, but if you do not publish, your scholarly career collapses. Of course, having published by no means implies that you do not perish. But if you aspire to a career in academia, you have to publish, and the more, the better. This, in short, is an illustration of contemporary academia's iron cage.

Publish or perish has become known far beyond the confines of academia. It comes as no surprise, then, that a variety of articles in popular media implement the theme in wider discourses in the English-speaking world (Aitkenhead, 2013; Colquhoun, 2011; Kristof, 2014) and in Germany (Könneker, 2018; Pörksen, 2015). However, publish or perish is far from being coherent. Not only is it referred to by different names but it also appears as an abstract imperative, as the most prevalent principle of a productivity and management regime in institutionalised academia, or as the current culture of scholarly communication in general. Publish or perish may be used as a referent to an age (Rosa, 2010: 55), an aphorism (Rond and Miller, 2005), a climate (Relman, 1977), a culture (van

Dalen and Henkens, 2012), a doctrine (Moosa, 2018: vii), a *Fluch* (German: curse; Könneker, 2018), a *Grundgesetz* (German: constitution; Barth, 2019: 13), an ideology (Vannini, 2006), a mantra (Guraya et al., 2016), a phenomenon (Miller et al., 2011), a slogan (Hexter, 1969), a syndrome (Colpaert, 2012), or a system (Lee, 2014).

If an individual wishes to be a scholar, they have to submit their scholarship to the terms of this competition. These terms dictate that what 'matters in academia are publications' (Harvie, 2000: 115). In classic sociological terms, we may think of the transcendence of commodification to explain this. A publication comprising scholarship in text appears to be a trivial thing. Its authorship is a name reference in discourse, placing it within a tradition. It has a use value in the communication of scholarship: by being published, text is made visible to an audience that aspires to engage with that scholarship. 'But, as soon as it steps forth as a commodity, it is changed into something transcendent' (Marx, [1867] 1906: 82). The publication – stepping forward to compete formally – no longer just communicates scholarship. It assumes the commodity form and is in competition with all other commodities on terms of marketability in institutional accumulation, on terms of comparability in a job market, and no longer merely on terms of use in discourse. The dissemination of ideas from author to reader and the potential competition of ideas *after* dissemination are substituted by the competition of ways of dissemination and the fact of dissemination in the first place. Its value is the referenced formal authorship. Such authorship as a commodity form means a predominance of the symbolic over the material, a 'mystical character' (Marx, [1867] 1906: 82) that does not originate in use value. The exchange value of authorship as a commodity form dominates over the use value of scholarship in discourse.

We might, polemically, claim: how else is scholarship to be communicated? How can others engage with a scholar's thinking if that scholar does not publish? An answer could be: by means of teaching, by oral dialogue, by sharing informal text. But this can be neither marketed nor efficiently counted. The once normative ideal of the unity of teaching and scholarship as conceived by Humboldt – his conception of *Bildung* – is replaced by preference for the new – the ideology of innovation – in which output needs to be countable and marketable as individual instances.[2] Originality becomes meaningless where it is seen not within its contextuality but as information as suggestive advertisement. The intrinsic complexity of dialogue – in teaching, in conversation, and in the contextuality of text – is to be resolved in the abstracting, formal instances of information that can be accounted for efficiently. This ideology results in a 'mad run rush for more publications' (Rosa, 2010: 55) in which every formal representation of something new is worth more than the capacity of advancement of rational discourse or the development of intellectual competence and daring. The abstract production of marketable output replaces the substance of a contribution, that is, produced formal authorship replaces the communicating text: the 'desire to produce knowledge, to share ideas, and to make an important contribution, is just one impetus for academics to publish. It may, however, no longer be the primary one' (Hyland, 2015: 6). As more intrinsic scholarly motives vanish, this is lamented as the *perversion of authorship* (Barth, 2019: 13). This perversion is an increasing disbalance of formality and substance.

Historically, the university and its clusters of disciplines are often characterised by a variety of dichotomies: idiosyncratic versus nomothetic, understanding versus explaining, historical-hermeneutical methods emphasising the subject versus exacting methods of objectification, qualitative versus quantitative paradigms, and so on. These terms are significant for respective cultures, carrying symbolic patterns that guide actions and signify worldviews. They are also often positioned to symbolise the opposition of the humanities and the sciences. In this role, they are overly generalising, trying to encompass a range of disciplinary practices that are hard to unify. Still, they offer an approach to understanding: a starting point for further, more specific enquiry.

For characterising the contemporary university in this sense, one particular dichotomy may be that of the comparable, formal output that signifies new information versus idiosyncratic, qualitatively complex, and intrinsically non-formal scholarship. The wording already indicates the difficulty of referring to this dichotomy. Nevertheless, it seems essential for answering the question of what the point of publishing is. It helps us to understand the

---

[2] In fact, the 'Czech Republic and [the] UK show the lowest percentage of institutions balancing teaching and research' (Bruni et al., 2020: 1132).

constitution of publishing practices in the humanities. This dichotomy is the new public management (NPM) notion of valuing measurable output above substance.[3] It is research versus teaching – the production of something new versus the passing on of that which is known. That which is new needs to be signified in the form of authorship. Publishing, in this understanding, is a means to turn scholarship – its idiosyncrasy, complexity, and requirement of qualitative engagement – into publications that yield formal authorship. It is driven by a competition that emphasises the auditing of individuals in their production of this – definite, marketable, and efficiently measurable – output. Against an ideal understanding of publishing as a means of communication, the empirical reality of publishing needs to be seen as a distancing of both the scholar subject and the intrinsic communicative purpose of text.

How can the grounds for this and its praxis be understood? How can the ambiguity in the categorical publish or perish be explained? How does the Weberian dichotomy of substantive and formal rationality help? How can the impact of the REF on publishing practices be understood? This book provides answers to such questions by outlining what it means to publish and how this meaning is distanced from an intrinsic motivation of contributing to scholarly discourse. It picks up the many concerns voiced in academia. These are, foremost, articulated in the day-to-day conduct, in the life-worlds of both early-career and senior scholars who wish to focus on an intellectual agenda, but have to respond to the alienating governance principles of competition on formal output.

Methods and Empirical Data

This book is an empirically grounded critique of publishing practices. I investigated these practices during several empirical studies, the results of two of which are published for the first time in this book. They enable readers to comprehend publishing practices in their institutional context,

---

[3] In short, NPM refers to the governance principles of public institutions that are ambiguously characterised by 'free market rhetoric and intensive managerial control practices', as discussed by Lorenz (2012: 600); see also Bacevic (2019: 101) and Münch (2011: 96–121).

how scholars perceive those practices, and what challenges there may be. This book is decidedly short. I focus on the scholar as an author. This focus serves two purposes: it provides researchers and policymakers with a concise introduction to what authorship and publishing in the humanities mean today; and it creates a starting point for future research that integrates and looks at particular aspects of authorship and publishing more comprehensively, particularly their materialist impact. Therefore, this is not a book about technical aspects of writing or publishing. It is also not a book about publishers, or about bibliometric quantifications of authorship. It is a book that puts forward a contextual understanding of publishing practices to explain the empirical situation of authors in the humanities.

The empirical data of this book are based on two studies: a quantitative survey conducted in 2018 and a set of qualitative interviews carried out in 2019/20.[4] Both of these studies take place within a case study frame that employs scholars in Germany and the UK as subjects that actualise the practices in question. The two countries are comparable in terms of size and scholarly institutionalisation. However, they are unique in particular characteristics: German academia is governed by a tremendously conservative career system, while the UK has a rather progressive but strongly hierarchised career system; Germany shows efforts to manage excellence nationwide, but only a few institutions are addressed by this management of excellence and it has little impact on publication practices in general, while the UK's efforts to manage excellence seem all-encompassing and are intricately intertwined with publications; German humanities scholars, who are very much culturally bound to a (Humboldtian) traditionalism and thus find the new governance practices and demands to internationalise something of a shock, are generally dismissive of having to use the English language and publish in non-traditional English journals, while UK scholars, who have never been strongly bound to Humboldt and are (by discursive default) rooted in academia's lingua franca, English,

[4] I conducted these studies as part of my doctoral research at University College London. This research was funded by the Arts and Humanities Research Council UK (AHRC) through the London Arts and Humanities Partnership (LAHP) as well as the Studienstiftung des deutschen Volkes (German Academic Scholarship Foundation).

seem better equipped to navigate the internationalist drive. This list is, of course, just an abstract. I do not endeavour to explain in depth the two countries' characteristics. Rather, I employ the two countries as a frame for analysing different manifestations of the governance of scholarly work.

Quantitative Survey

The survey was exploratory in nature. Its aim was to reach sufficient number of scholars to allow for a comparison of the two-by-two matrix of the humanities and the social sciences in Germany and the UK. The questionnaire was online between April and July 2018, and 1,177 scholars participated in the survey. Clearing from the responses disciplines other than the humanities and the social sciences, as well as emeriti scholars, left an effective sample of 1,017 scholars. Figure 1 illustrates the distribution of responses for the full sample.

Career positions in Germany and the UK are not easily comparable since positions have different names and careers progress differently. The most striking difference is perhaps the tenured professorship in Germany. Alongside this are a bulk of scholars in the large cluster of the German *Mittelbau* (which often includes a whole range of positions from the postdoc to just below tenured professorship). Some of these scholars form the German *Privatdozent* (untenured senior scholars); others, a rather small number, are the *Juniorprofessoren* (often younger than *Privatdozenten* but sometimes with the option of tenure). The rest make up the mass of the *Wissenschaftliche Mitarbeiter* (literally: scholarly employees). This stratified career system is substantially different compared with the UK's rather progressive – in the sense of more linearly hierarchised – system. I will discuss more of this as we go through the book. Table 1 shows the distribution of survey participants across these groups.

To get an idea of what the abstract terms of career positions mean, the following four scatterplots (see Figures 2 and 3) show the distribution of scholars' active years for each cluster of the two-by-two matrix.[5] Active years refers to the respondents' own statements about how long they have been active in academia, in absolute numbers. The three middle clusters

---

[5] Detailed statistics can be found in the Appendix.

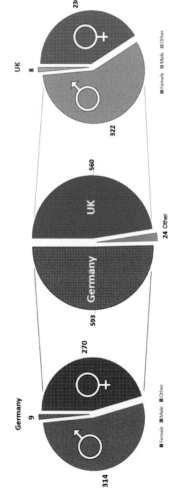

Figure 1 Distribution of participants in quantitative survey.

Table 1 Effective sample of quantitative survey.

Germany		Doctoral student	Wiss. MA	Juniorprof.	Unten. senior	Tenured prof.	Subtotal	Total
	Humanities	17	148	34	52	106	357	545
	Social sciences	14	86	26	18	44	188	
	Humanities	5%	41%	10%	15%	30%		
	Social sciences	7%	46%	14%	10%	23%		

UK		Doc	Junior	Mid	Senior	Subtotal	Total
	Humanities	13	94	80	61	248	472
	Social sciences	13	89	66	56	224	
	Humanities	5%	38%	32%	25%		
	Social sciences	6%	40%	29%	25%		

Excluded total: 160

All: **1,777**

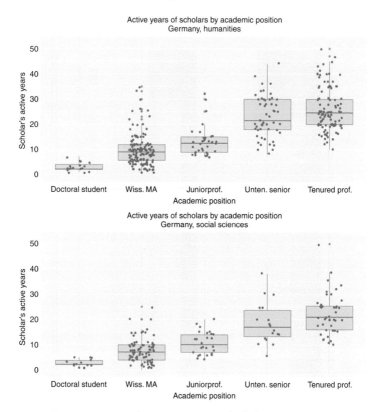

Figure 2 Active years and career positions of scholars in Germany.

make the *Mittelbau*. As can be seen, they are distributed across a wide range of years. Tenured professors are comparable to their untenured colleagues in terms of years of experience. Career development in the UK seems to be more hierarchical: the junior-, mid-, and senior-level groups indeed represent a progressive system. The junior professorships and the tenured professoriate in Germany disturb such linearity.

Figure 4 further shows the correlation between the scholars' ages and their self-identified active years in academia. Germany is very linear with a high

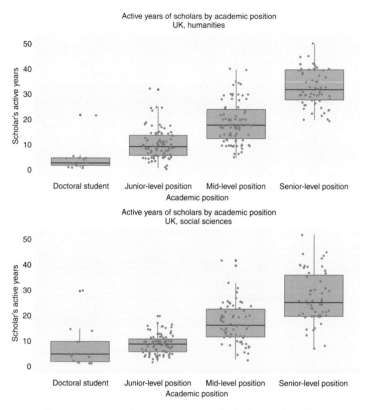

Figure 3 Active years and career positions of scholars in the UK.

correlation. The UK shows greater variation, especially as the system seems to be more permeable: quite a few scholars access a career at a higher age. German academia seems to be less hospitable for such permeability: either you are in from an early age on, or you are out. This is a quantified statement of Germany's rigid career system.

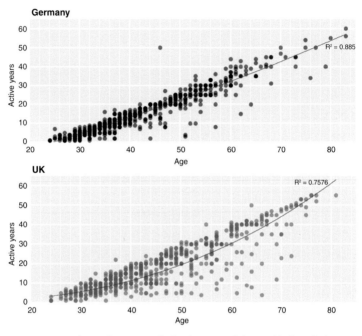

Figure 4 Correlation between scholars' ages and their self-identified active years in academia.

Who Are Humanities Scholars?

This book is about the humanities. However, who are humanities scholars? Rather than engaging in epistemological or historical discussions of what the humanities are – a discussion that is surely worthwhile in itself – the disciplinary designation employed in this book is based on the more worldly method of self-identification. Within the quantitative survey, scholars were asked to designate themselves regarding both their discipline *and* their scholarly cluster. This allows us both to identify differences between the humanities and the social sciences, between Germany and the UK, and to appreciate how scholars see themselves within academia.

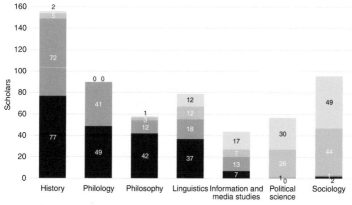

Figure 5 Identification of scholars as either humanities or social sciences, within select disciplines.

All representations of the following data rely on this self-identification of the scholars, that is, how the surveyed scholars themselves attribute their scholarship to a broader cluster. This book, therefore, does not engage in defining disciplines or clusters; rather, it looks at the humanities as a – perhaps, at times, contradictory – whole. It is about HSS – that is, about the humanities and social sciences as a united cluster – only insofar as it employs a matrix in which the social sciences are a reference group. For key disciplines, the intersection of disciplinary understanding and broader clusters is illustrated in Figure 5.

Table 2 provides an overview of the distribution of the most often stated disciplines within respective groups, which allows us to account for potential biases.[6] These are the most important disciplines as they represent at least two-thirds of all respondents, often even more.

---

[6] To be read, for instance: 29 per cent of the Juniorprofessor respondents self-identifying as humanities scholars are historians.

Table 2 Distribution of selected disciplines by career position in percentages of total within a group.

Germany humanities

Discipline	Wiss. MA	Juniorprof	Unten. senior	Tenured prof.
History	22%	29%	17%	21%
Archaeology	8%	3%	6%	8%
German philology	6%	6%	12%	9%
Philosophy	11%	6%	15%	8%
Linguistics	12%	0%	6%	8%
Literature	5%	3%	2%	3%
Theology	4%	9%	2%	5%
Art history	3%	9%	12%	1%
Classics	1%	0%	6%	5%
English philology	1%	3%	0%	4%
Law	2%	0%	4%	2%
Of total	76%	68%	81%	74%

UK humanities

Discipline	Junior	Mid-level	Senior
History	31%	23%	26%
Archaeology	7%	10%	5%
German philology	1%	3%	0%
Philosophy	7%	4%	3%
Linguistics	6%	4%	11%
Literature	5%	4%	7%
Theology	4%	4%	3%
Art history	2%	4%	2%
Classics	5%	1%	7%
English philology	7%	13%	8%
Law	2%	1%	2%
Of total	74%	69%	74%

Germany social sciences

Discipline	Wiss. MA	Juniorprof	Unten. senior	Tenured prof.
Sociology	22%	19%	22%	9%
Communication	7%	12%	11%	18%
Geography	0%	0%	0%	0%
Economics	5%	15%	11%	11%
Education	8%	12%	0%	0%
Political science	15%	23%	6%	9%
Linguistics	6%	0%	17%	5%
Law	3%	12%	0%	11%
History	3%	0%	6%	0%
Management	2%	0%	0%	11%
Of total	72%	92%	72%	75%

UK social sciences

Discipline	Junior	Mid-level	Senior
Sociology	13%	15%	16%
Communication	2%	2%	4%
Geography	7%	5%	9%
Economics	8%	3%	5%
Education	2%	3%	9%
Political science	14%	11%	11%
Linguistics	6%	9%	0%
Law	6%	11%	11%
History	1%	0%	0%
Management	7%	8%	13%
Of total	65%	65%	77%

Table 3 Effective sample of qualitative interviews.

		#	Level	Gender	Discipline
Germany	University	1	Non-senior	Male	History
		2	Non-senior	Female	Philology
		3	Senior	Female	History
		4	Senior	Male	History
	"Excellence University"	5	Non-senior	Female	Philology
		6	Non-senior	Male	Philology
		7	Non-senior	Male	Philosophy
		8	Senior	Male	Philology
		9	Senior	Male	Philosophy
UK	University	10	Non-senior	Female	History
		11	Non-senior	Female	Philosophy
		12	Senior	Female	Philology
		13	Senior	Male	Philosophy
	"Excellence University"	14	Non-senior	Female	Philosophy
		15	Non-senior	Female	Philosophy
		16	Senior	Male	History
		17	Senior	Male	Philosophy
		18	Senior	Female	Philology

Qualitative Interviews

The results of the survey are complemented by a series of semi-structured, qualitative interviews. These provide the crucial contextual knowledge we need to understand the lived experiences of the scholars. I conducted eighteen interviews in person or via phone during winter and spring 2019/20. I chose the interviewees in an iterative process; they represent an equally balanced range of career positions from core humanities disciplines from both Germany and the UK. I transcribed and anonymised the interviews, then coded them twice using NVivo,[7] resulting in nearly 600 different code snippets. For the mark-up coding,

[7] NVivo for Windows by QSR International. File version: 20.4.0.4.

I followed a qualitative-thematic approach to highlight internal meaning structures within themes. Table 3 provides an overview of the effective sample.

Structure of This Book

I proceed in four chapters in this book. Firstly, I look at basic characteristics of publishing practices. This will provide answers to questions such as: how much does a scholar publish? What do they wish for their future monograph(s)? And how is open access (OA) perceived? This is a statistically driven outline that will result in a humanities publishing persona.

Secondly, I look at the matter of publishing pressure. The core of this is to clarify who experiences what kind of pressure and what are core strategies for dealing with it. This also outlines how publish or perish can be understood more comprehensively.

Thirdly, I look at the UK's REF in comparison to the German *Exzellenzinitiative*. The REF highlights how governance principles are negotiated and become manifest in the role ascribed to publications.

Lastly, I draw together the preceding concrete empirical discussions to form both an outline of the constitution of publishing practices and an abstract conception of the societal value of the humanities in the context of their communicative practices.

2 How and How Much Scholars Publish: Basic Characteristics of Publishing

This chapter provides basic data about how much and what scholars publish as well as how they themselves perceive key characteristics of their publication practices. It will give a feel for the empirical situation of publishing and serve as a reference guide. The empirical situation is highly relevant as it shows the numbers of publications at respective career positions. The chosen representation showcases the similarities and differences between Germany and the UK as well as between the humanities and the social sciences. Critiquing publishing practices and shaping policies – institutional or country-wide – requires an appreciation of what actually happens.

Next to basic numbers relating to published artefacts, this chapter also concerns questions of the predominance of single authorship, language use, and popular books. These complement bibliometric studies of the self-identification of authors. Moreover, the various figures and tables go beyond numbers evidencing the sizes of publishing portfolios, so that how these portfolios are constructed will become clearer in more than quantitative terms. The imagined backward-looking scholar with their dusty books on endless library shelves seems to be a stubborn *gestalt* representing a traditional humanities scholar. Some of the following survey items ask how scholars perceive themselves to enable a better understanding of, for instance, the use and perceived value of metrics, the use of self-publishing services, rapid or unhurried publication processes, the importance of physical copies being available in libraries and bookshops, and online discoverability. This is followed by a discussion of OA.

How Much Do Scholars Publish?

An essential question is how much is being published at what career positions. The following figures showcase this. Figures 6 and 7 indicate the considerable differences within average portfolios of published articles and monographs. Published output rises in line with career progression. In Germany, there is a clear division between senior and tenured scholars. Moreover, within both the humanities and the social sciences, there is a distinction between the number of publications of tenured (Germany)

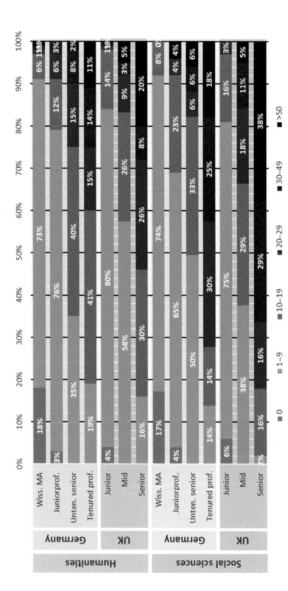

Figure 6 Numbers of published articles in scholarly journals by career position.

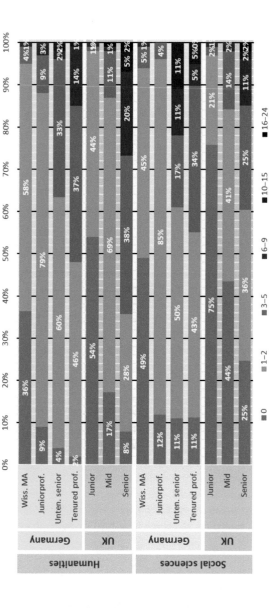

Figure 7 Numbers of published monographs by career position.

and senior (UK) scholars in that scholars based in the UK tend to have more articles published than scholars in Germany. This difference is similar for published monographs.

Figures 8 and 9 are detailed representations of scholars in the humanities and their numbers of publications by clusters of years instead of by career positions. Scholars in Germany tend to have fewer articles published in the early years of their careers. In the clusters from Year 16 onwards, this shifts, and German scholars have more articles published than scholars in the UK. While the latter seem to progress more linearly, there is a clear break in the development of published articles among German scholars.

There is a similar tendency in the early years in terms of monographs, but the break happens earlier. Scholars in the UK on average publish more monographs in the earliest stage of their careers. However, from Year 5 onwards scholars in Germany publish more monographs. This development progresses steadily. Scholars in the UK seem to publish more monographs only at later, perhaps more secure stages of their careers.

Figures 10 and 11 show data about published contributions to edited volumes (or collections) and editorships. These tend to be more important in the humanities than they are in the social sciences, as the data confirm. There are also more contributions published and edited by scholars in Germany. An explanation for this is the formal requirement about grants and proceedings in Germany: the *Sammelband*, which I discuss more concretely in Chapter 4, is increasingly perceived as a burden. Witness here also the differences between tenured and untenured seniors in Germany.

Figure 12 shows information about textbooks. It confirms the general assumption that this format is published in much lower numbers in the humanities and social sciences than in other non-HSS disciplines; only a few senior HSS scholars have published one or two textbooks, and rarely do these scholars publish more than five textbooks.

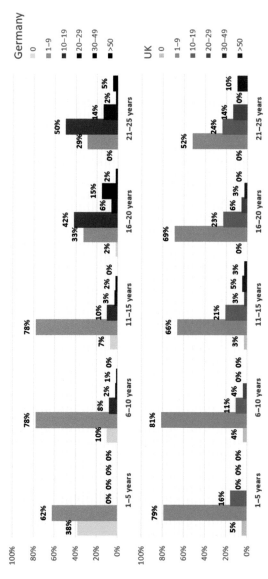

Figure 8 Numbers of published articles in scholarly journals, grouped in clusters of years active in research.

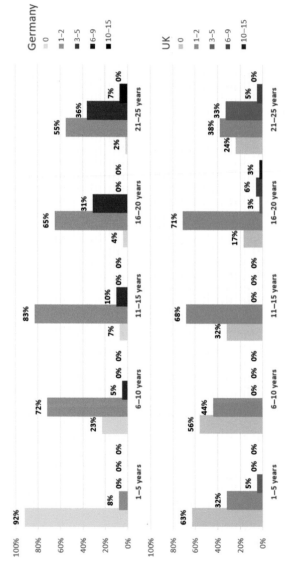

Figure 9 Numbers of published monographs, grouped in clusters of years active in research.

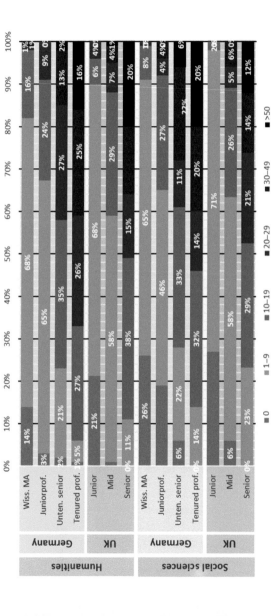

Figure 10 Numbers of published contributions/chapters by career position.

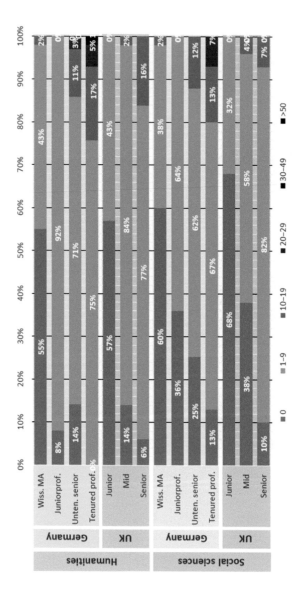

Figure 11 Number of editorships of edited volumes.

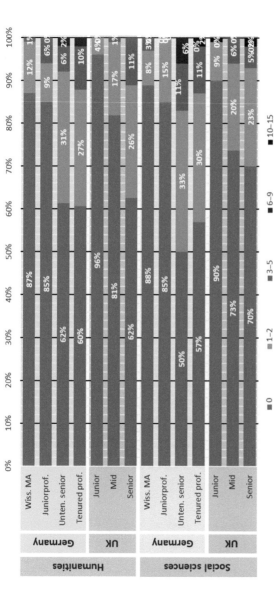

Figure 12 Numbers of published textbooks by career position.

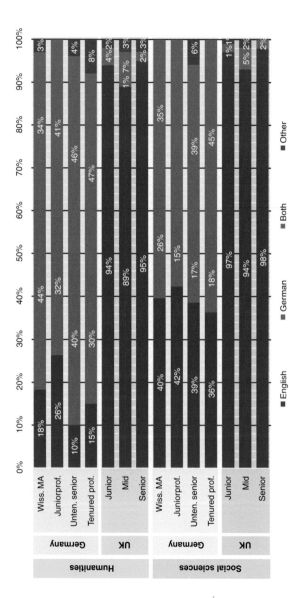

Figure 13 Languages used in scholarly publications.

What Languages Do Scholars Publish In?

Figure 13 provides an overview of the use of languages in scholarly publications. It is evident that English is most influential in the UK. But also among German scholars, the English language seems to be an important medium, in the social sciences more so than in the humanities. In particular, a mix of English and German becomes predominant with increasing seniority. Languages other than English or German seem to be rarely used; it is mostly tenured humanists that use them in Germany.

Figure 14 provides further data about language use in a follow-up to the preceding question about whether the language mostly used is a second language. The data confirm that many scholars in Germany are making use of a second language (I discuss more of the issue of internationalisation in the context of the *Exzellenzinitiative*). However, the number of scholars doing so is quite high in the UK as well, more so among junior than among senior scholars. An explanation for this may be the diversity and internationality of early-career scholars gaining scholarly experience in the UK.

What Other Formats Do Scholars Publish In?

Figure 15 shows that only a fraction of scholars have published non-scholarly books related to their scholarship. In general, the number of scholars having done so rises with increasing career levels, but there are exceptions. Other non-traditional publications are shown in Table 4. Policy and grey literature publications were the most mentioned genres followed by a variety of article formats for non-scholarly discourses.

Figure 16 shows data about blogging practices. As with non-scholarly books, the number of scholars who write a blog is quite low overall. Blogging is clearly more popular in the UK than it is in Germany. Moreover, blogging is not confined to younger scholars; many senior scholars seem to publish blog posts regularly, especially collective blogs.

Further Publishing-Related Perceptions

The following figures provide data about perceptions of publishing-related issues such as authorship and metrics. Figure 17 shows the significant difference between the humanities and the social sciences in terms of

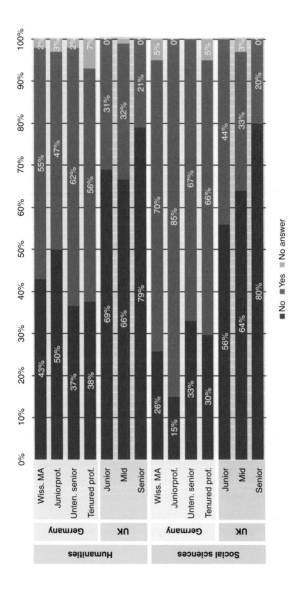

Figure 14 Second languages used in scholarly publications.

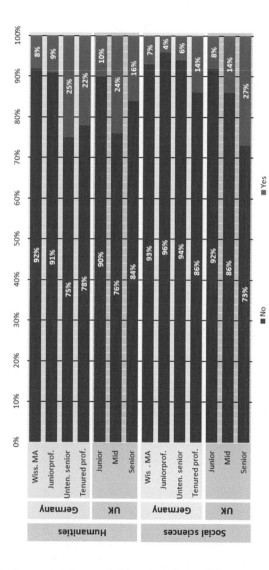

Figure 15 Popular books dealing with scholarship.

Table 4 Other non-scholarly publications in use.

Type of non-traditional	Mention	Type of non-traditional	Mention	Type of non-traditional	Mention
Policy report or grey lit.	31	Newsletter	3	Commentary	1
Special interest journal	30	Conference proceeding	3	Jubilee book	1
Newspaper	26	Interview	2	Own edited volume	1
Digital resource	23	Radio	2	Pamphlet	1
Magazine	16	Schoolbook	2	Paper for my employer	1
Various online	16	Animation	1	Preprints on ResearchGate	1
Video content	15	Archive	1	Print on demand	1
Own or project website	14	Arts practice	1	Project Atlas	1
Curatorial work	9	Audiobook	1	Self-publishing on Amazon	1
Engage in fora	5	CO-authored multigraph	1	Subtitles	1
Brochure	3	Comics	1	Translation of poetry	1
Ebook	3				

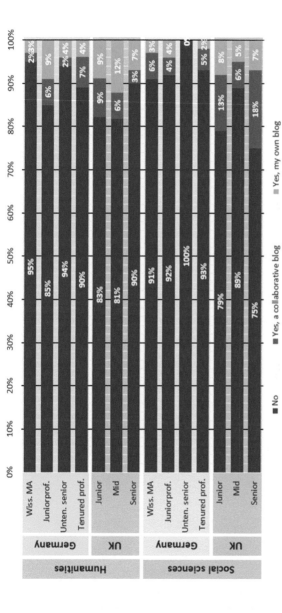

Figure 16 Number of scholars blogging on a regular basis.

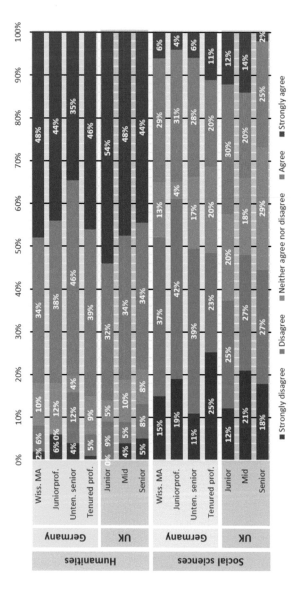

Figure 17 Predominance of single authorship (in one's own area/discourse).

authorship: single authorship is defining in the humanities; it is much less so in the social sciences. This confirms the common assumption that the humanities predominantly rely on sole authorship.

Figure 18 further indicates assumptions about the connection between metrics and research. An overwhelming number of scholars, especially in the humanities (75 to 90 per cent), but also in the social sciences (50 to 70 per cent), (strongly) disagree with the statement that their research can well be expressed in quantifiers or metrics. This confirms assumptions that scholarship in the humanities as well as in wider areas of the social sciences seems ill-suited to being expressed in quantifiable terms.

Figures 19 and 20 further indicate differences between disciplines: humanities scholars seem to be less knowledgeable about metrics than social scientists are. Disagreement with the statement about having knowledge of metrics is higher among humanists as well as among Germans, and also increases with seniority. In regard to format, the differences between social scientists and humanists is larger for journal articles, especially in Germany. This points to a confirmation of the assumption that there is less engagement with metrics among the traditionalist German scholars than there is in the UK.

Connecting these items with the preceding one, the question has to be raised as to why scholars indeed follow metrics, for there are more scholars indicating that they do so than there are scholars who claim that metrics are representative of their scholarship. Since articles and books are representations of scholarship, it seems that scholars follow metrics not to understand fellow scholars' perceived value of their scholarship but to understand a use value of publications that may be disconnected from scholarship.

The responses displayed in Figure 21 indicate that there is a difference in the prevalence (or awareness) of *salami slicing* (publishing least publishable units of one's scholarship): it seems to be less the case in Germany and also less so in the humanities.

The last item in this row shows that there is strong agreement with the statement that a publisher's brand is an important indicator for quality while browsing through a bibliography (Figure 22). Nearly half of all scholars at least agree with this statement, with humanists in the UK and social scientists in Germany reaching agreement rates of up to 80 per cent. This confirms the often-hypothesised claim that brands are taken as crucial heuristics. However, the rates vary unsystematically.

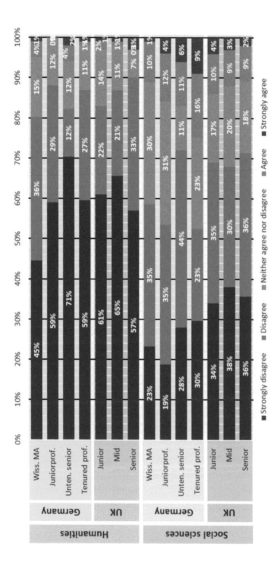

Figure 18 Perceptions of whether the value of research can be expressed in quantifiers/metrics.

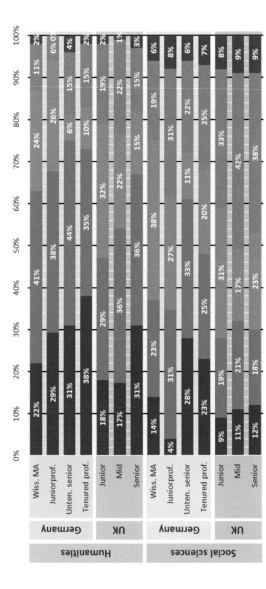

Figure 19 Knowledge about metrics of one's published monographs.

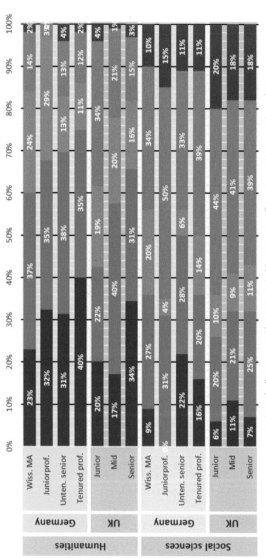

Figure 20 Knowledge about metrics of one's published articles/journals.

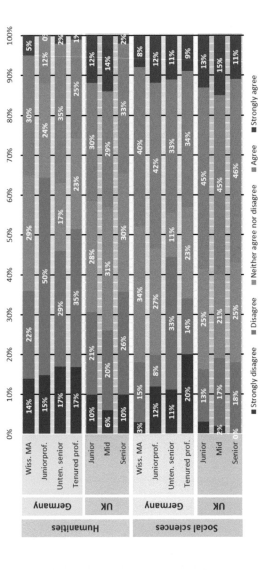

Figure 21 Pervasiveness of salami slicing/making as many publications as possible out of a single analysis or finding.

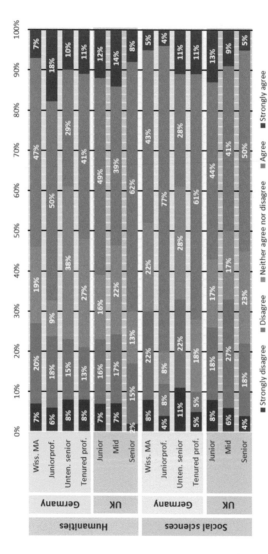

Figure 22 Employing the publisher's brand as an indicator of quality.

Specific Monograph-Related Needs

The following items look at what is important for humanities scholars when considering their next monograph. To begin with, there is a strong rejection of self-publishing services across disciplines and countries (Figure 23), though the social scientists seem to be a bit less reluctant. This is accompanied by a high rate of missing information: many scholars seem either to not know about such services or to be unsure about engaging with them.

Figures 24 and 25 both relate to temporal aspects of publication processes. Importance here is given to the connection: the former statement connects a fast publication process to mere immediacy, while the latter connects an unhurried publication process to content improvement. There is a perceptible division between the humanities and the social sciences. Especially for the humanities, it is evident that an unhurried publication process focussing on content is more important than rapid publication. Though their tendencies are comparable, humanists reject rapid publication processes more than social scientists do. In return, humanists show higher rates of assigning importance to unhurried publication processes, and Germany more so than the UK.

The necessity of monographs being available in physical form in libraries is confirmed by – especially senior and tenured – humanities scholars (Figure 26). Only a small fraction reject the perceived importance of the printed book being on library shelves. The social sciences show less need of such physical availability.

Figure 27 mirrors this in that it enquires about digital discoverability. There is widespread agreement that this is crucial or considerably important, though social scientists are even more strongly concerned with it than humanities scholars. The two figures compared show that for humanists, especially in the earlier career positions, digital discoverability is even slightly more important than physical availability.

Figure 28 shows the perceived importance of monographs being available in bookshops. This item shows quite mixed results. There is a tendency among German scholars to emphasise this importance more than UK colleagues do. Responses to this item indicate that, compared with online discoverability and physical availability in libraries, bookshops are seen as being the least important places for circulation across disciplines.

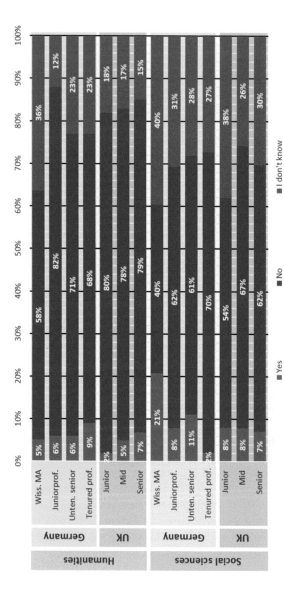

Figure 23 Use of a self-publishing service ('I would publish my next monograph with a self-publishing service').

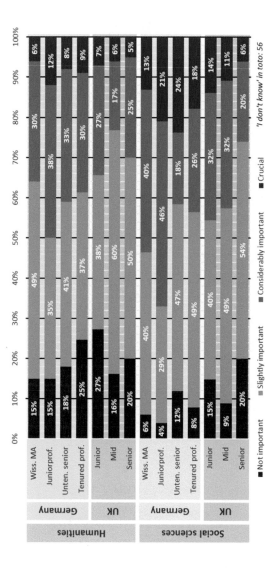

Figure 24 The importance of rapid publication processes (for the next monograph).

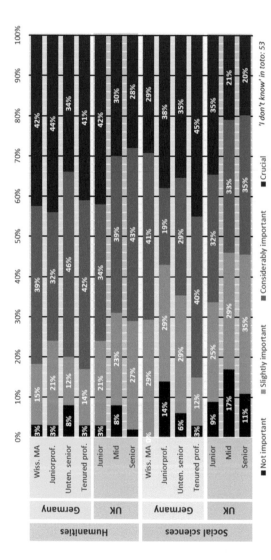

Figure 25 The importance of unhurried publication processes (for the next monograph).

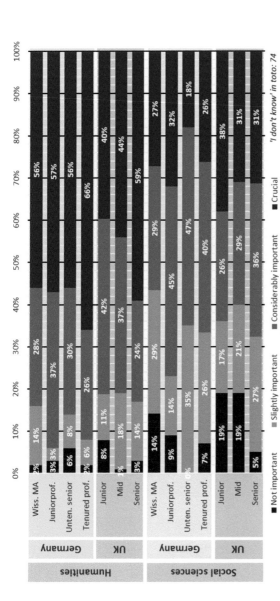

Figure 26 Importance of monographs being available in physical form in libraries (for the next monograph).

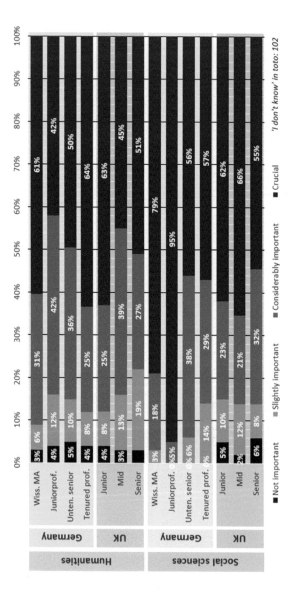

Figure 27 Importance of monographs being discoverable online (for the next monograph).

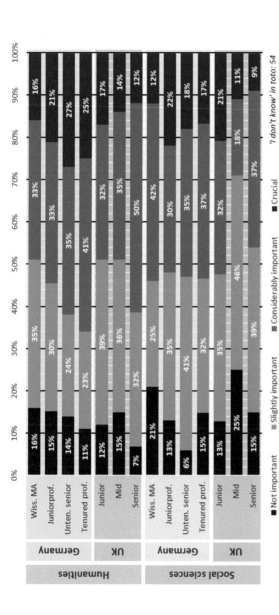

Figure 28 Importance of monographs being available in bookshops (for the next monograph).

The UK Humanities Publishing Persona

The preceding data provide a fruitful basis for determining key characteristics of publishing portfolios and perceptions that can be summarised to
evoke the material manifestation of an average humanities scholar. This can
be thought of as a persona: a representation that highlights decisive features.
As it is built on averages, however, it must be used with caution.

The personal portfolio of a scholar in the UK comprises high output at
early-career positions, particularly in terms of articles. They publish early at
high rates. The first monograph is also published early. Mid-career progress
is made steadily. This is different among German scholars whose output
shows a clear break beyond which they seem to reach a more secure plateau
with a steady, higher output of both monographs and articles.
I contextualise this in the subsequent chapters; the numbers here provide
an early abstract idea. The break in the German development is decisive,
falling within the time frame of attaining a secure position. This break also
coincides with decreasing publishing pressure, as I discuss in Chapter 3. In
relation to the steady development of UK scholars stands the notion that
pressure to publish is also more distributed across careers, instead of
focussing on early years, as is the case in Germany. In terms of contributions to edited volumes, the German scholar is considerably more engaged
than the UK scholar. This, too, reflects what I discuss later as a problem of
the German *Sammelband*: the blind output of contributions without much
audience.

The situation regarding use of different languages is predominantly
illuminating for German scholars. And it highlights the – expected – low
diversity of languages in use in the UK. However, while it can be assumed
that the German scholar who publishes in English makes use of a second
language, it is worth reflecting on the use of second languages among
scholars in the UK, too. One in three junior and mid-level scholars and
one in five senior scholars make use of a second language in the UK. It
shows that a language advantage for *the UK scholar* is rather relative since
simply *being institutionalised* at a UK department – thus, counting as
a scholar in the UK – does not necessarily mean being a native speaker.

In terms of publication characteristics, the data showcase that the bibliographic claim of the predominance of single authorship is confirmed by many a scholar in the humanities. Note that this does not reflect epistemological necessity. This is the perception of scholars, which can be translated as: I see mostly individuals communicating. Collectives in dialogue seem rather invisible. The average scholar in the humanities only rarely checks the development of their metrics; younger scholars do so more than senior ones. Still, there are more scholars who do so than there are scholars who consider metrics to be reflective of the value of their scholarship. Despite this being rather abstract, it is instructive for our further discussion of governing scholarly work. The UK humanities scholar considers strategising content for publications in terms of publishing a least publishable unit, known as salami slicing; the practice is not as established as in the social sciences, but it is more so than with their German colleagues. Irrespective of discipline or country, at least one in two scholars deploys the publishing brand as an important indicator in bibliographies.

Among the four groups studied, the humanities scholar in the UK is the least likely to make use of a self-publishing service for their next monograph. The UK scholar is also most decisive about this. Rapid publication processes are mostly not important. A noteworthy difference between Germany and the UK is that the German scholar wishes for an unhurried publication process more than the UK scholar. In terms of availability and discoverability, the humanities scholar wishes for both the print copy in libraries and digital discoverability online. These are by no means exclusive, but the difference to the social scientist is instructive. The latter has rather mixed feelings about the printed copy but is almost relentless in demanding digital discoverability. Perceptions are much closer among humanities scholars. However, they unite with the social scientists in being undecided about print copies being available in bookshops: there are only a few more humanities scholars who claim that this is important, and a few more social scientists who reject its importance.

All of this provides an initial understanding of publishing practices in the humanities. Though these mostly concern material manifestations, the persona showcases key differences between clusters of scholarship and countries. To be sure, there remain open questions such as: what is the least publishable unit in the humanities? Is the single author a relict of the practice of tradition and routine or grounded in methodological self-understanding? This book is not the place to answer such questions, unfortunately, though it does provide an informed starting point for further explorations.

Open Access

Another key issue to be discussed in this chapter is OA. The matter of openness is accorded a more prominent position here since it is among the most debated issues in scholarly communication in the UK. I first look at data before going into a more nuanced discussion that will highlight the ambiguity of this debate.

Figures 29 and 30 show the experience of having at least one article or monograph published as OA.[8] The differences vary and there is no consistent tendency. Most striking – but also most obvious – is the difference between genres: scholars have more experience with OA articles than with monographs. While more UK scholars have experience with OA articles (particularly social scientists), more German scholars have published an OA monograph compared with UK colleagues (again with the highest rates among social scientists). For both genres, overall experience with OA rises with seniority in the humanities in Germany. It decreases in the humanities in the UK (!). Moreover, since this is such a rudimentary issue to enquire about – the *one* publication experience with OA – it seems revealing to see the high numbers of those who have yet *no* experience with OA.

This empirical situation may be compared with Figures 31 and 32, which show the importance of OA for a scholar's next monograph as well as the experienced pressure to publish OA. The first item resulted in strong opinions. Among humanities scholars, there seems to be rather a rejection of OA, especially among senior scholars. In the UK, a stunning 43 per cent

---

[8] Note that the mode of OA is not specified here, leaving it to the common understanding of scholars. The qualitative interviews showcased that this usually means Gold OA.

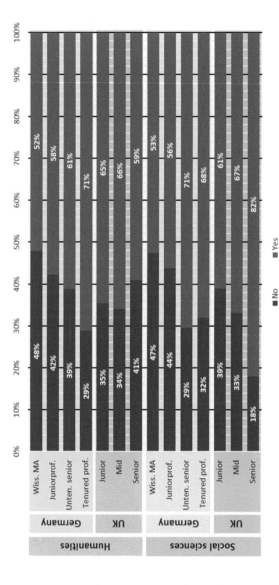

Figure 29 Article OA publishing experience, regarding at least one published article.

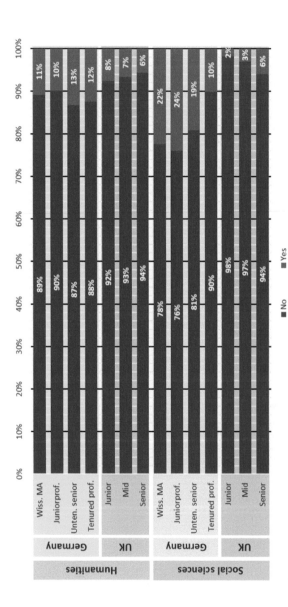

Figure 30 Monograph OA publishing experience, regarding at least one published monograph.

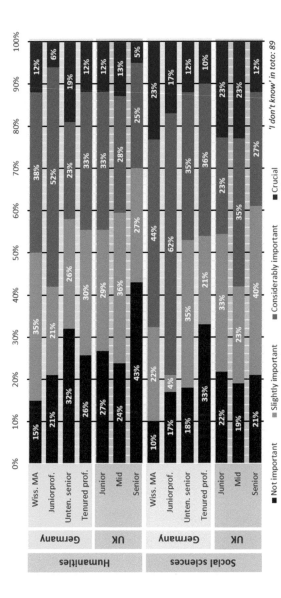

Figure 31 Importance of publishing OA (for the next monograph).

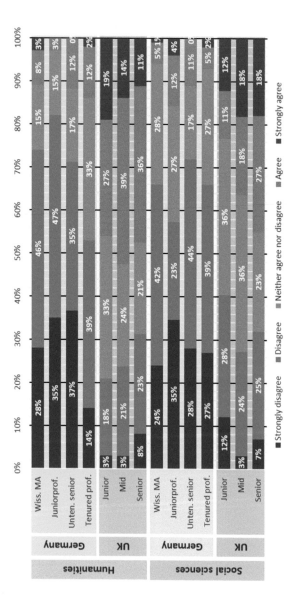

Figure 32 Pressure to publish OA ('I feel pressured to publish open access').

of senior scholars even claim that OA is not important at all. This is the highest negative result in the series of items about needs for future monographs in the survey overall. This indicates that OA is the least demanded characteristic for future monographs among – particularly senior – humanities scholars in the UK.

Figure 32 represents the experienced pressure to publish OA. Scholars in the UK indicate substantial perceptions of such pressure. It is largely rejected entirely in Germany. The country-specific differences are striking for this item.

It can be read from these data that pressure to publish OA is of considerable concern to about half of humanities scholars in the UK. They experience pressure yet, all the while, they indicate that they would not see it as important for their future monographs. This may be put in relation to the statements obtained from the qualitative interviews. These exemplify this ambiguity as both the need for justified equality *and* the voiced impression of unjustified institutional enforcement. Thus, OA appears to be perceived as a generally good measure in the wrong manifestation.

On the one hand, there is the force of a moral argument that allowing anyone to access publications freely is only justified. The taxpayer argument – meaning that scholarship funded by public investments should also be accessible to the public – is sometimes invoked. Besides this driver of societal justification is a common claim in favour of more widespread access to reduce tendencies of monopolisation. Rising costs and shifted library budgets alongside new investment demands in the form of journals, subscription programmes, and monograph series tend to reduce or fractionalise access. Scholars claim that it does not seem right that only wealthy colleagues can read all the new scholarship while others cannot, or have to wait for embargo periods to end.

On the other hand, and despite such claims, almost all interviewees have substantial reservations about how OA is institutionalised in the UK. Many perceive OA to be Gold OA with an 'author pays' model. This mere switch of paywalls from readers to authors – even in the form of their institutions as funders – only shifts the problem of accessibility. Some scholars further mention the problem of underfunding in the humanities. It is not the place here to discuss whether this claim is justified or only disguising perception. Either way, it fares as a social fact among interviewed scholars that they express reservations about providing capitalist institutions with substantial shares of the – perhaps only experienced – already scarce funds. This is related to the perception among scholars that there are many new and genuine OA venues that are – from the perspective of the scholar – mostly just that: new and open. The motivation of scholars in such cases seems to be to remain with the traditional journals as these are the main communicative sites of their discourse communities, potentially complemented with an archival manuscript. Publishing with one of the new, open journals seems to be out of question. These journals are open, but they hardly reach the desired audience. Moreover, in the light of being judged on formal authorship, the value of the brand – the name attached to the publishing venue – counts, too. These aspects are common to scholars in both Germany and the UK.

The substantial difference between the two countries is in experiencing systemic pressure as well as the source of such pressure. Scholars connect this to the REF in the UK. As I further discuss, the REF often fares as a discursive denotation, but its direct impact is actually funnelled through wider practices of meaning-making (such as how institutions or discourses translate abstract guidelines into subjective demand). One such practice – the ubiquitous discourse on the political demand of OA – results in a backlash against OA alongside a feeling expressed as pressure. It appears in this context as an alienating mechanism that divides the abstract idea of equality and its manifestation in the UK, so that opinions shift to negative positions.

The milestone reference works in this respect (Crossick, 2016; Finch, 2012) offer clear accounts of the politicisation of OA in the UK. Demands for openness in the UK Research and Innovation (UKRI) OA policy only reinforce this impression (UKRI, 2021). The continuous claims of underfunding and the discourse on Plan S in the UK are only the latest instances in this discursive row (see, for instance, British Academy, 2019; Eve, 2019a, 2019b; Royal Historical Society, 2019). The end of it, however, is not yet decided as publishers, funders, and institutions have to find suitable paths forward, especially in material terms.

This shows that the debate around OA is muddled with inconsistencies and ideological shallows. A complex of moral claims is often implied but not realised (Bacevic and Muellerleile, 2017; Knoche, 2019; Knöchelmann, 2021a; Natale, 2019). The *Budapest Initiative* formally laid the ground for a moral argument on a global scale, justifying OA by claiming to 'share the learning of the rich with the poor and the poor with the rich' (Budapest, 2002: n.p.). This is opposed by the appropriation of OA by capital, an appropriation that reduces said moral justification to mere rule-following in the sense that OA is not primarily a mechanism to share and allow for broader participation in discourse; rather, it exists to reinforce a scholar's or an institution's discursive power. The claimed democratisation of knowledge – even theoretically a difficult concept in the context of the contemporary university – becomes impossible in praxis (Knöchelmann, 2021b).

The fight against such appropriation by capital finds its place once again in bottom-up approaches. The vocal advocates position the agenda as one of liberating the governance of communication by fostering small, community-owned infrastructures (Adema and Moore, 2018; Barnes and Gatti, 2019; Moore, 2019). This shows valuable signs of progress towards more transparent and freely accessible communicative resources. But this agenda approaches scholarly practices, a social problem, with technical infrastructure. The motivation to make use of it needs to correspond to audiences. Technology alone can only partially change mindsets and motivations. The wrong governance – enforcement with an indifference to moral justification – can even impede this change.

Thus, OA needs to be seen in the context of this muddled ground: an ideologically heated debate, capitalist appropriation, ever-rising funding costs, and a policy regime that enables a mode of governmentality. The effect among individuals is a set of ambivalent impressions. There is a perceived policy-induced rule-proceduralism that claims to change publishing practices for the better. All the while, there is the demand for scholars to publish openly to foster their own reputations – and those of their institutions and nations. The opposition of *openness for marketable improvement* that has to be individually funded and the *socially better publication* constantly lingers within this set of ambivalent impressions in the UK. It evokes the contradictory appearance of a publicly accessible private knowledge product.

German scholars indicate much less of such pressure. The *Exzellenzinitiative* as well as funders have mostly only recommendations on offer; OA is not as politically enforced as it is in the UK. This may by no means be read as evidence that OA is unequivocally favoured in Germany. It may only mean that there is much less of a policy-induced debate (yet) in the humanities. And among those where OA is a topic, it still appears much more as *the good thing if others do it*. Indicative in this respect is a recent study which confirmed that OA has a subordinate role on the individual level, much behind reputation and peer review quality, in the humanities in Germany (Ambrasat and Heger, 2020: 26).

This appearance also reflects the issue of too little engagement with the question of what openness may mean in the humanities, and how the various layers of the debate are to be integrated. Attention to matters of an *open humanities* that can face the discourse on *open science* on par is either not given or shifted towards debates of digital humanities (Knöchelmann, 2019). But digital humanities is a discipline on its own, comprising its own epistemological principles and particular worldviews. It is unlikely that it will solve the problems of the humanities (in general) in today's digital world.

The need of an own discourse – termed *open humanities* or not – is in this light also a shelter against being *included* in open science, or being submitted to a digital epistemology of the digital humanities. There is a need for more transparency in humanities discourses and wider, more accessible distribution of its texts that is entirely independent of claims to become more digital in general. Even very traditionally working philosophers and philologists – developing their ideas with pen and paper, surrounded by printed books – can publish a preprint of their final manuscript or opt to change editorial practices towards more transparent modes of review. If they lack the skill of digital publication, it might become institutional practice to allow librarians or similar information service staff to arrange the digital publishing. This, however, is a question not of digital humanities but of motivation and culture.

Most of all, new means of openness should not appear as an add-on, a practice or technology that is to be used in addition to established practices. There is no need for more content to be published. Much rather, the reorientation of communicative practices towards smaller communities with qualitative difference instead of symbolic hierarchies may allow breaking with the rush for more publications. A requirement for this is the balancing of niche and relevance – of being both specific and relevant for a scholarly community without falling for the allure of rankings and hierarchical relevance. A short excursus on what this means will form the last section of this chapter.

Venues, Discourse Communities, and Consecration

The value of formal authorship and its correspondence in audiences can only come about by means of venues. Venues are the media that execute and signify the transformation of text into publication, and that make this signified text visible to an audience. The term *venue* serves here as a denotation of an individually branded site of publishing (often also referred to as *publisher*, *outlet*, *imprint*, or simply *brand*), may it be a journal, a publishing house, or a distinct monograph series within a publishing house. This allows a perspective on the mechanisms of venues across different genres from journals to books. A brand functions in a similar way irrespective of the genre it refers to: it is the denotation of a publication venue to its symbolic and material value produced and reproduced in practice. A venue may generate visibility, confer esteem, or indicate inclusion in a discourse community.

The act of publishing a text includes it in the tradition of a venue. Inclusion and exclusion of venues means inclusion and exclusion of both community and its discourse. By means of its active and passive selection of content, the venue enables the construction of coherent discourse and community membership. The boundaries of discourse are negotiated via publishing: epistemes, forms, methodologies, languages, reference styles, and so on. In short, what is discussed, how it is discussed and in what ways it is presented is continuously developed and reproduced through publishing practices, in circular reflection with practices of readership. This can be a qualitative differentiation.

In praxis, however, being within a certain community or discourse – having published with its media – or being reviewed there constitutes an added value.[9] As venues are employed as heuristics in a (ranked) hierarchy, the value of signposting qualitative differentiation turns into a symbolic sign of quality per se. This is a notion of quality as encountered in a single market; all have to submit to an impossible ranking of being better, and not of being different. Seeing a venue as a heuristic for hierarchy evokes its added value, which may be regarded as an aura.[10] It is, thus, worth publishing at a venue not because it constitutes the audience of a publication but because it constitutes the appearance of an authorial scholar. It is the scholar who benefits from this publication irrespective of their communicative engagement with an audience. The mark of *being published* with a journal is the primary success. Having published at a venue constitutes the visibility and membership that allows for future potential, too; it is a Matthew effect that becomes exacerbated as venues and authorship are accorded more and more value. Those who are visible will be made more visible.

When Bourdieu asks 'who is the true producer of the value of the work[?]' and 'what authorizes the author[?]' (Bourdieu, 1980: 263), he is relating to such mechanisms of consecration and legitimisation as are constituted by social belief. A community's members dialectically authorise a venue and its content through the repeated engagement with that venue's publications; they collectively objectify scholarly work. This results in the institutionalisation of a medium as a respected venue. Authorship and publishing practices, in this sense, produce and reproduce the consecratory value of venues and the content they publish.

If a venue is positioned high up in a hierarchy of quality – the high-impact journal or publishing house – it assumes a certain eminence. The venue prophesies that *this is worth reading*, which, after a while, constitutes part of the quality itself – a self-fulfilling prophecy in the Mertonian sense (Merton, 1948). The text becomes legitimised by social belief where this belief has 'consequences' that make reality conform to the initial belief' (Biggs, 2009: 295). A relatable example is that arguments put forward by well-known scholars

---

[9]   It is this value that is often referred to as symbolic capital in Bourdieu's sociology (Bourdieu, 1998: 85; Bourdieu, 2013: 294).

[10] One may think here of the Benjaminian aura of works of art (Benjamin, [1935] 2010: 15).

are perceived as being more apt and, because of this, the audience is more inclined to believe and build on them (as opposed to arguments made by more obscure scholars). This is a 'self-confirming process, making for the greater evocative effect of publications by eminent men of science' (Merton, 1968: 62).

The statement that *this has been peer reviewed* plays a similar role as it works as a heuristic today. It signifies that this is *real scholarly content*. And yet, the applicability is not as profound a legitimator as it is in, for instance, the life sciences. The dialogical recursion of discourse in the humanities is a long-term review mechanism in itself. Peer review is not necessarily assumed to be a reliable mechanism or indicator. And yet, humanities scholars repeatedly claim that some kind of filtering is required for assessing colleagues or applicants so that peer review increasingly also assumes the role of a legitimate signifier. This filtering, however, is not dominantly connected to a consequent hierarchisation of venues (as in terms of Journal Impact Factors in, again, the life sciences). Rather, a sort of clustering emerges that is not necessarily a strict hierarchy. Certain venues have a reputation that symbolically legitimises content (after having constituted its material existence), while other venues do not achieve such a reputation (and thus their provision of material may or may not remain somewhat irrelevant for discourse).

Only some venues manage to resist serving as a reductive tool of efficiency: the niche venues that fly under the radar of any attribution of excellence. These often constitute existential sites of niche discourses in the humanities. Scholars within these discourses seem to appreciate such venues as being communicative refuges. This shows the importance of the diversity of small publishers in the humanities: the manifold venues that allow the regional and topical specificity of discourses and communities. Expression of visibility plays an important role here; it is a visibility that can hardly be accounted for within the generalising single market of national excellence. The seemingly symbolically minor venues provide a valuable ground for the existence of that niche. *Being there* with one's scholarship *is the value*, despite the missing symbolism of external reputation. This, in short, explicates a character of use value in the humanities that – against the mystical character of exchange value – appears to be mythical in the context of global excellence.

This needs to be a key consideration for the debates on OA. As long as venues are employed as heuristics in a hierarchy – heuristics that move away

3 Publish or Perish: The Empirical Reality of the Pressure to Publish

What are drivers of the pressure to produce more and more publishing output? The easy answer is competition. However, competition can take place in manifold ways. It could be a matter of substance and qualitative difference. As scholars highlight, though, it rather takes place on the basis of comparative output. The way competition takes place – the narratives and governance behind it – is abstracted in its terms. These, instead of competition per se, are responsible for the pressure to produce publications since they build on the recognition of qualitative work in formal terms. This shows the circularity of competition that invokes the self-referentiality of output.

Who experiences this pressure? What are the strategies for dealing with it? What does the balancing of contributing to discourse and producing output mean in praxis? This chapter provides answers to such questions. I first look at what *publish or perish* and competition mean, then investigate the empirical reality in quantitative terms, before discussing how this can be interpreted, comprising insights from the qualitative interviews.

Publish or Perish, Competition, and Efficient Filtering

Publish or perish is an ambiguous term. On the one hand, it refers – in both discourse and praxis – to the terms of competition in academia, in particular how publishing output is preferred to intellectual development. Publishing practices and the focus on formal authorship embody *publish or perish* in this sense. On the other hand, ideology is negotiated among those affected in everyday discourses – particularly early-career scholars. They reinforce the impact of *publish or perish* by extending its narrative. It solidifies the principle that formal authorship really *is* the objective of publishing and the primary way to enter an academic career. As this everyday discourse – chatter at conferences, philistine management advice, the rhetoric of constant improvement and excellence – is passed on among young scholars, the terms of competition become reified. Reducing *publish or perish* to a single, context-unspecific denotation would mean disavowing parts of its force.

Looking at this issue from its very basic conditions, we might say that, practically, being a scholar means having a job today. You *work as* a philosopher (or historian or philologist, etc.); you do not have to *be* one existentially. To be sure, you can be a philosopher without a position at a research institution. Your philosophy might even be a vocation rather than a job today. But it will be much harder to make a living on this philosophising. The scholar with a (paid) position at a university is *allowed* to engage in intellectual practices as their primary occupation; this is even more the case if the position in question is a research position that allows engagement in practices of *knowledge production* without (or with the reduced) need to teach others elements of the existing body of knowledge. Such a research scholar is paid to engage in intellectual practices. To continue to do this, they have to prove their intellectual productivity. The question here is how is this productivity defined? What *is* intellectual productivity? And why does intellectual ability seem to be defined primarily in terms of formal output? These are questions pertaining to the terms of competition in the job market.

Competition, abstractly, seems inevitable in academia, especially in a – potentially future – academia that is democratically governed. Competition, in a benign, small-scale market, can be thought of as a qualitative appreciation. It can even be seen as a beneficial mechanism in the sense that it kindles qualitative advancement and the potential for diversity. Such competition also diminishes the destructive aspects of networks and exclusive circles. Rational discourse in search of the better argument needs to be seen as a competitive process. Competition is a means of filtering that is tied to the specificity of that which is to be filtered. It turns into an adversarial mechanism if it stops being a means that is specific to substance and begins to be an end in itself, an end towards which substance begins to align.

Widening participation illustrates the problem of increasing competition on the wrong terms. Demand for more democratic access has been translated as allowing potentially anyone access to the institution in question irrespective of background, if only they showcase a certain merit. This alludes to the ideal of meritocracy – a wolf-in-sheepskin ideal as originally conceived satirically by Young (1994).[11] Such a widening of participation also

---

[11] Meritocracy until today fulfils its function of disguising problems of social mobility and democratic means to higher education, as several recent contributions to this discourse show with different lines of arguments; see Mandler (2020);

takes place among aspiring scholars in both Germany and the UK, and increasingly also among mid-level and senior scholars in the UK. The filtering of scholars with merit and those without is treated as needing to be ever more efficient; it is an unintended consequence of widening participation. The more there are to compete, the more efficient the terms of competition need to be. Correspondingly, formal representation of achievement needs to be comparable. At the same time, the products they compete on become more and more tied to a single market of ranked products that need to be available in time, irrespective of whether those producing them are early-career or senior scholars. On the one hand, students and scholars need to do ever more to achieve a head start in the race or secure their position. On the other hand, each dimension in which they can compete becomes exploited and signified by comparative symbol; merit becomes a formal dimension.

Socially desirable democratic access, thus, can result in negative consequences. This compares to the development of capitalism that turned the substance of small markets and their modes of competition into a single market. Where there are many local markets, their differentiated and respective terms are *opportunities* to engage. These opportunities turn into *imperatives* as the market structures unite and align, and all those who engaged in differentiated structures are suddenly compelled to engage in a single one. Inclusivity and differentiation turn into force and alienation depending on the market that shifts *opportunity* to *imperative*. As a consequence, the 'existence of market dependent tenant-producers' creates 'competitive pressures' (Wood, 2016: 130): 'pressures to produce cheaply, pressures that reinforce ... the cost-sensitivity imposed by already existing imperatives of competition' in recursion (Wood, 2016: 140).

Instead of allowing many small, qualitatively differentiated markets that foster individual intellectual development, the scholarly market in which individuals compete during early careers is marked by unifying terms. Scholars become alienated from the work they conduct; their scholarship

Markovits (2020); Sandel (2020). Especially helpful is the culture argument in Karabel's (2005) monumental study, which shows the fluidity of what merit can denote—or can be made to denote.

becomes a means for competing on the currency of authorship where it should be a basis for qualitative appreciation. The output produced becomes alienated from its communicative purpose in scholarship and dialogue. This is a mode of recognition and reward that is reductionist and creates a Weberian social closure.[12]

Prominent in targeting this is Münch, who relates to such reductionist mechanisms at several instances in his analyses of modern German and Western academia. He determines forms of social closure as markers of achievement that are set in terms external to scholarly discourse, in a unifying market that is constructed on efficiency. Among such terms are rankings and metric-based performance measurement (Münch, 2007: 73–160), which overemphasise a rhetoric of marketable reputation (such as of *world-leading* or *excellence*) (Münch, 2008: part 2), or the creation of an audit university where strategic, external management of quality replaces the autonomous conduct of scholarship, research, and teaching (Münch, 2011: 94–123). Rankings, marketable reputation, and the governance of external strategy in research management mean increasing competition. As Münch (2007, 2008, 2011) shows, this competition does not work in favour of intellectual development.

The alienation resulting from this is experienced as a mode of hypercompetition. The empirical situation of this is also well captured in the wider literature. Precarious employment further allows institutions the freedom to *let them compete* until the most productive scholars remain. The certainty of a secure position appears to become ever harder to obtain for the individual. Witness the

---

[12] Social closure means that communities can become closed to outsiders by setting the standards of prestige, status in a hierarchy, race, or material wealth. The community encloses itself by closing relationships within the community based on the markers of distinction and, thus, defining the social other as outsider. Reproduction of hierarchy and status are secured against outsiders. Such 'stratification by status goes hand in hand with a monopolization of ideal and material goods or opportunities', as Weber originally suggested (Weber, [1922] 1978: 935). That is, in the context of the REF, obliviousness of social closure fundamentally hinders equal chances in a free market and instead enforces a gradual monopolisation.

difficult employment situations of aspiring scholars in Germany (Agarwal, 2015; Pauli, 2016; Sander, 2017; Ullrich, 2016, 2019) or the UK (Acton et al., 2019; Anonymous academic, 2018; Calkin, 2013; Swain, 2013; White, 2015). In both countries, there are ever more PhDs accompanied by fewer long-term prospects of academic employment (Maher and Sureda Anfres, 2016). A stunning 87 per cent of scholars in the German *Mittelbau* are on fixed-term contracts (Ambrasat and Heger, 2020: 5), and only 4 per cent of an annual doctoral cohort has the potential to reach a permanent position in academia (Wissenschaftsrat, 2014: 25). Add to this, particularly for the humanities, the tales of unemployability of PhDs or how it is considered a failure to leave academia (Kruger, 2018; Segran, 2014), and look at the mental health crisis pervading academia, and even worsening, for young scholars and researchers in the Western dominion (Anonymous editorial, 2019; Evans et al., 2018; Levecque et al., 2017). This all describes the 'precarious position of young scholars' with its 'nasty, vicious circle' of poorly paid, short-term positions that deprive scholars of the security to develop and publish truly original scholarship (Beard, 2019: n. p.). It is, thus, argued that academia works on hypercompetition (Moore et al., 2016: 8) which is articulated by the rhetoric of achieving excellence but, ultimately, is said to harm research quality. It is even claimed there is 'a Darwinistic competitive race among (especially young) academics – for funds, citations and publications, not for better crafted and more convincing (counter)arguments' (Vostal, 2016: 105). Moreover, output regimes in the form of performance measurement reinforce negative effects and stress (Franco-Santos and Doherty, 2017). And, most recently, a major study conducted by the Wellcome Trust showcased again the devastating research culture that scholars in the UK experience. Seventy-eight per cent of scholars agree with the statement that 'High levels of competition have created unkind and aggressive research conditions', and expectations of security and longevity in career prospects have dropped to the lowest levels among early-career scholars (Wellcome Trust, 2020: 15–16).

These terms of competition are embodied by publishing practices. To compete means to publish. It means to be compared to others by means of formal authorship of published scholarship. This results in the empirical reality of pressure-inducing output regimes. This pressure is what is visible in the data that I collected through my survey.

Who Experiences Pressure?

The data provide a comparative lens on publishing pressure in Germany and the UK. The data presented in Figure 2 are valuable in this context. They show that careers seem to be more linearly hierarchised and progressive in the UK. There are also more similarities between the humanities and the social sciences. This relates to the progressive and, as it were, more universally competitive nature of the career system in the UK. Permeability (Figure 3) also requires competitiveness. This is different in Germany where the system is characterised much more by a hierarchy focussing on the end of a few tenured professorial chairs with a bulk of non-professorial mid- and senior positions. The path of professorship is mostly decided quite early on during the competitive years of building the foundations of a career. These decide whether, eventually, a tenured position will be within reach or not. This is especially visible with the *Juniorprofessorships* that are positioned to replace the traditional *Habilitation* in Germany. It pushes for increased competition at an even earlier time in the career, often about five to ten years after the PhD, or at the age of about thirty-five. This is said to be a problem in the humanities since intellectual maturity requires more time instead of such an early rush towards hastily proving competitiveness (Brechelmacher et al., 2015: 24–5). This is visible in the data as the early-career scholars are quite close in terms of age, while the senior clusters are rather loose and wide-ranging.

I conducted an in-depth analysis of variations in the pressure to publish within the quantitative data of my survey. The result is a clustering of humanities scholars in relation to their experienced pressure.[13] Looking at

---

[13] For this, I clustered humanities scholars' responses to the questions *I feel pressured to publish more journal articles* and *I feel pressured to publish a monograph*. This resulted in three distinct clusters: *no pressure* comprises all those respondents who indicated only strongly disagree, disagree, or neither agree nor disagree; *low pressure* comprises all those respondents who indicated agree for at least one of the two questions, but no strongly agree; and *high pressure* comprises all those respondents who indicated at least once strongly agree. These pressure clusters exclude doctoral scholars to focus on those with at least postdoctoral experience within the academic system.

these pressure clusters (Figure 33), it seems that the appearance of career positions (Figure 2) is turned upside down. Germany becomes the progressive case as experienced high pressure is very much focussed on early-career positions, advancing to the more loosely defined low pressure clusters. No pressure is experienced by a diverse, though decidedly senior group of scholars. Experienced pressure is much less focussed in the UK. German groups show standard deviations of 6.44 and 9.55, and means of 10.32 and 15.96 for high and low pressure, respectively; the UK shows standard deviations of 7.62 and 11.12, and means of 13.54 and 19.58.[14] This already anticipates the correlations to be explored subsequently: namely that pressure in the UK is not so much an early-career pressure (getting on a path to a tenured position) as it is a universal pressure that also impacts scholars in more advanced positions. Think of how the REF may induce pressure more loosely around early to mid-career positions in the UK. In Germany, where such a mechanism does not exist, pressure is concentrating on *getting into a long-term career* as such, and so focusses more on the earlier stages of a career.

Figures 34 and 35 show how career positions and gender are distributed in pressure clusters. While the majority of senior and tenured scholars experience no or little pressure, experience of pressure to publish is pervasive among earlier career positions. Moreover, the experience of forms of pressure is higher among women than among men. Witness that the share of those experiencing low pressure is about half in all career positions. The differences stem from distributions of no or high pressure.

Table 5 shows the distribution of disciplines within pressure clusters, for selected disciplines with the largest shares. This is an indicator for understanding the share of disciplines within pressure clusters. Since analysis of the level of individual disciplines does not have sufficient statistical power, this component analysis is the best option.

Figures 36 and 37 provide further details about the experience of pressure. These representations show how the clusters relating to experienced pressure to publish are built, in groups of years. In terms of journal articles, the pressure overall is very high. However, experienced pressure

---

[14] The detailed statistics can be found in the Appendix.

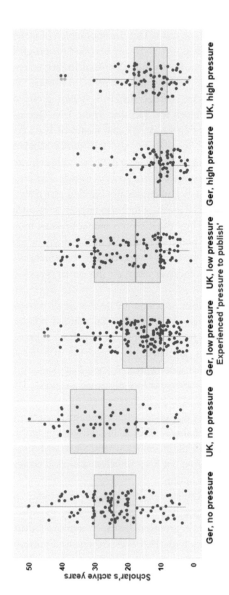

Figure 33 Experienced pressure to publish in the humanities – comparison between Germany and the UK.

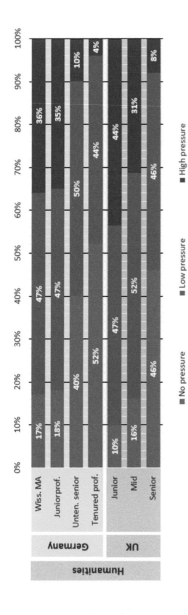

Figure 34 Distribution of career positions in pressure clusters.

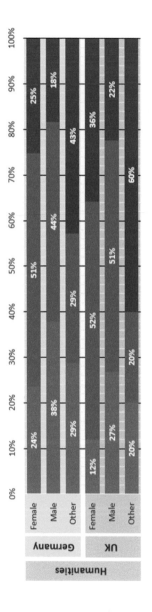

Figure 35 Distribution of genders in pressure clusters.

Table 5 Disciplines within pressure clusters.

Distribution of selected disciplines by degree of pressure to publish, Germany humanities			
Discipline	No pressure	Low pressure	High pressure
History	15%	29%	13%
Archaeology	9%	6%	5%
German philology	12%	6%	5%
Philosophy	5%	12%	19%
Linguistics	10%	10%	11%
Literature	5%	3%	4%
Theology	4%	3%	8%
Art history	2%	4%	6%
Classics	5%	2%	0%
English philology	5%	1%	0%
Of total	71%	76%	71%

Distribution of selected disciplines by degree of pressure to publish, UK humanities			
Discipline	No pressure	Low pressure	High pressure
History	20%	26%	33%
Archaeology	6%	8%	7%
German philology	0%	2%	1%
Philosophy	2%	5%	7%
Linguistics	8%	6%	6%
Literature	4%	5%	6%
Theology	2%	3%	6%
Art history	6%	2%	1%
Classics	8%	4%	1%
English philology	8%	10%	8%
Of total	64%	70%	76%

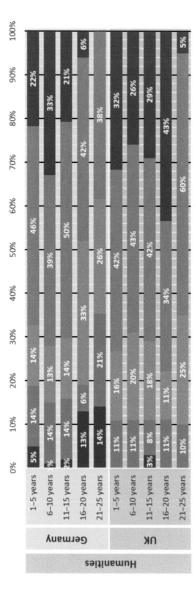

Figure 36 Pressure to publish more journal articles ('I feel pressured to publish more journal articles').

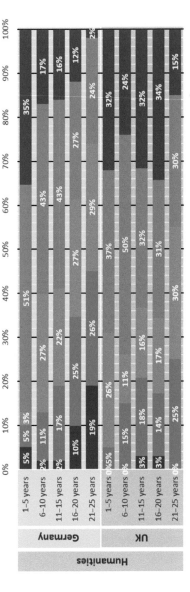

Figure 37 Pressure to publish a monograph ('I feel pressured to publish a monograph').

sharply declines after Year 15 in Germany, while it remains high in the UK and only the extreme experience declines. It is about this time that scholars in Germany have either tenure or a permanent position. The pressure remains high in the UK, perhaps considerably so, owing to institutional assessment demands.

In terms of monographs, the situation in Germany shows an unparalleled peak at the early stage and a clear decrease along career positions. In the UK, however, the pressure rises after Year 6, remains high, and only decreases after Year 20. Even then, it remains higher than the pressure experienced after Year 16 in Germany.

Figures 38 and 39 relate to the published portfolio, shown here again for the sake of comparison. Both correspond to the preceding representations of experienced pressure as well as to the subsequent graphs. The peaks and changes of experienced pressure are mirrored by the published portfolios.

Variations of Experienced Pressure

Next to mere prevalence of pressure, the data also include a perspective on experienced connections. The perceived pressure to publish is further investigated in relation to its temporality in Figure 40 (in groups of years active) and Figure 41 (in pressure clusters). Again, the overall amount of pressure experienced is much higher in the UK. Strikingly, while the experienced connection of temporal pressure and quality decreases over time among German scholars, it increases over the years among scholars in the UK. Especially those who perceive high amounts of pressure indicate a strong connection to temporality: more than 70 per cent of scholars in the UK experiencing high pressure at least agree that the quality of their research suffers as they feel pressured to publish faster.

Figure 42 shows that there is a considerable break in the prevalence of the wish to reduce article output in order to focus on a monograph. In Germany, this corresponds with the data already seen, with the break of experienced pressure at around the cluster starting with Year 16. In the UK, this break sets in earlier. In the context of the, likewise, fewer published monographs at the time of this break in the UK, this reinforces the interpretation of scholars experiencing being overburdened with demands

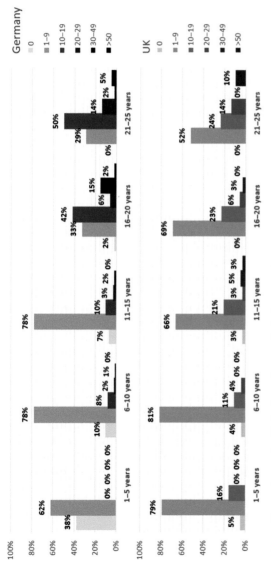

Figure 38 Numbers of published articles in scholarly journals, grouped in clusters of years active in research.

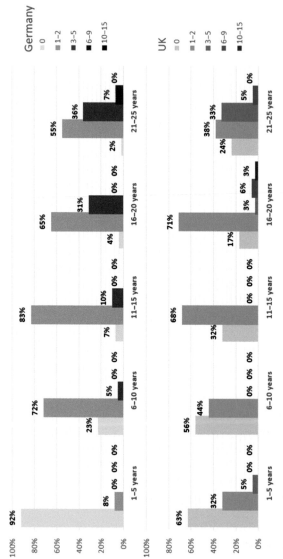

Figure 39 Numbers of published monographs, grouped in clusters of years active in research.

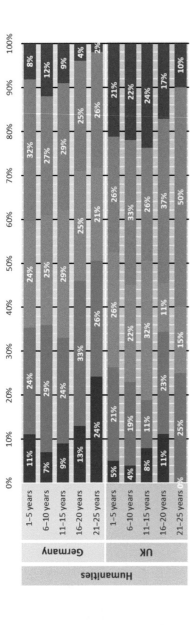

Figure 40 Pressure to publish faster in relation to quality ('I feel pressured to publish faster such that the quality of the research suffers').

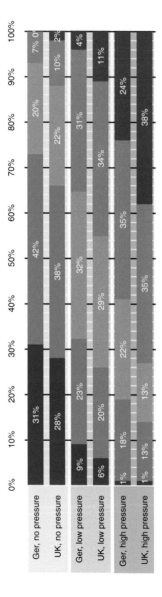

Figure 41 Pressure to publish faster in relation to quality ('I feel pressured to publish faster such that the quality of the research suffers'), in pressure clusters.

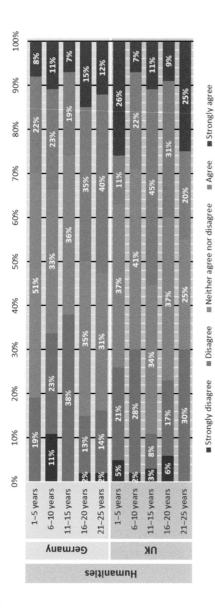

Figure 42 Wish to reduce article output in favour of a monograph ('If I had the choice, I'd publish fewer articles or contributions to focus on a monograph').

■ Strongly disagree ■ Disagree ■ Neither agree nor disagree ■ Agree ■ Strongly agree

for articles (in the light of the more intrinsic aim to capture one's scholarship in the longer form of a monograph).

Contextualising the data on pressure, Figures 43 and 44 are revealing in the way that they point to the over-satiation with articles. This experience is generally rejected for monographs, especially among early-career scholars (Figure 43). Turning to articles, there is a general consensus that there are too many being published (Figure 44).

Negotiation of Quantity and Quality

These representations fit in with the notion of an output regime in the context of uncertain futures. They show the systemic pressure experienced by early-career scholars. This takes the form of a bottleneck when it comes to entering a long-term career in Germany. In the UK, however, the pressure remains high over the course of progressing careers. Essential for understanding the reason for this is the REF, but only indirectly (as I discuss in Chapter 4). Scholars repeatedly reference the job market and application procedures – those instances setting the terms on which they have to compete – as direct reasons for their experiencing pressure to produce formal output. Trying to avert the uncertainty of uncertain futures under precarious contracts, early-career scholars do what appears to be the requirement of this job market. Insights from qualitative interviews provide the necessary contextual knowledge for further understanding strategies for dealing with uncertain futures. They are an insight into an allure of seemingly rationalistic alleviation.

In the course of strategising publishing, pressure is negotiated by balancing quality and quantity. It remains true that quality tops quantity. But as quality is difficult or even impossible to produce ad hoc for most (young) scholars, quantity can make up for lack of it. This is true especially for early-career scholars who have not yet had time to develop their intellectual programme. When temporal pressure to perform – such as the construction of an early publishing list – weighs on the early-career scholar, they may strategically choose to focus on the number of publications on that list. Several scholars explained this strategy of negotiation.

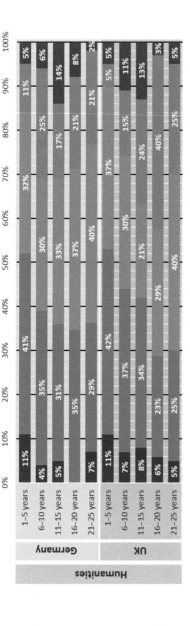

Figure 43 Perception of too many new monographs being published.

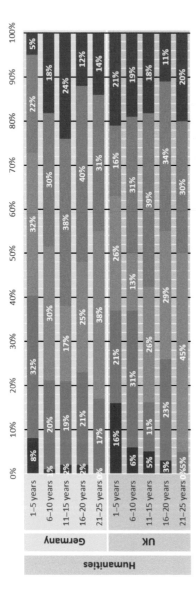

Figure 44 Perception of too many new articles being published.

Witness a philologist whose explanation is exemplary in this respect:

> [I]f you get into an evaluation then you'll have to have some high-quality articles since the content will be assessed – but then not the whole publication list – only the four [or] five texts that you submit alongside your list [will be assessed] – so then – yes this reflects some kind of hybrid strategy for those who work on their publication list – some for the length and some for the quality.

Negotiation of quantity and quality can be found in other statements as well. A single contribution to discourse may signify the ability to work in that subject area; several contributions to a single discourse, at best in different venues, signify additional expertise and raise the visibility of the individual in that discourse and its branches. In addition, this is preferably multiplied by contributions to different discourses. Quantity, thus, also means to broaden the appearance of one's abilities in the eyes of external assessments. It is claimed to be essential as a young scholar to be visible in the discourses – not in order to advance the discourse but to signpost that you can do the job, that you can produce relevant output.

Biagioli (2016: n.p.) states that some scientists 'aim high, but not too high', deploying all means to produce more publications – just not those high-impact publications. If publications do not *look too high-impact* (or appear in high-impact venues), it is unlikely that they will be scrutinised. Usually, only a few publications are required for closer inspection during application procedures, meaning that a few high-quality publications suffice for showcasing intellectual ability. This is what the scholars express in my interviews, too, only that discourse communities are more tightly knit in the humanities. Nevertheless, the interviewees suggest that a scholar has to go beyond those few publications to be scrutinised in job applications in the first place; those with more publications are said to fare better during the early stages of assessment. Grant applications even require *the five or ten best publications* of an applicant. But an early postdoc is hardly likely to have twenty publications to choose the best from. This creates the impression that they are not enough, as an interviewee explained. And it forces them to produce more.

The result is a stack of publications that is only partially driven by the intention to contribute to discourse – to *produce* knowledge – or to show-case intellectual ability. It is a fulfilment of the requirement to produce formal authorship which helps in the competition for places. Such publications do comprise scholarly text, of course. As Williams poignantly puts it in respect to publishing least publishable units, '[t]here are demands of academic promotion, which can encourage one to make as many published pages as possible out of whatever modest idea one may have' (Williams, 2008: 183). These demands enforce instrumentalisation so that early-career scholars learn to balance quantity and quality to yield the highest reward of formal authorship.

This negotiation of quantity and quality is crucial for understanding publishing in connection to the case that there are too many articles, and the claims that the overall quality of discourse is decreasing. It is obviously not the case that there are no good articles and that no one is intrinsically interested in the communication of scholarship. Much rather, established practices of authorship and publishing incorporate this negotiation of quantity and quality so that the communicative system seems overburdened; quality seems to decrease in general because the good cannot be seen among the many. The individual publication counts less as each scholar, and communities generally, produce masses.

The imperative to publish and the ways instrumental publishing practices respond to it are prevalent also in how senior scholars act in their roles as mentors or supervisors. Asked what advice supervisors or colleagues give to early-career scholars, almost all scholars in my study implicitly articulate the negotiation of quantity and quality, particularly as an issue of early formal output standing against a desirable intellectual development. This performative strategising, the structural pervasiveness of so doing, and even the possibility of its success as mere performance all indicate that the resulting publications are not driven by the desire to contribute to discourse. The resulting artefact – the formal list of publications – effects a symbol of individualistic achievement that is caused by competition on formal rationalistic terms. The formal list of publications overshadows the individual publication. This symbol is reflexive since publication lists and discourse about them reify and reinforce the terms on which they have come to existence. In the long run, thus, they become routinised, honing the valuation of individual achievement in academia to the level of efficiency that philistine management requires universities to run on.

This seems to make scholars in the UK more sober and even defeatist. In fundamental ways, they express the pressure to publish as a relentless pressure to perform. The pressure here is more strongly connected to institutional regimes than it is in Germany. The influence of the REF and auditing are emblematic. Most interviewed scholars were conflicted in this respect: they signified a sense of gloom and discomfort about the advice they give their early-career mentees alongside a sense of obligation or even burden that – since this is the way one *has* to behave in the job market – not giving this advice would be irresponsible. A philosopher in the UK summarises her advice thus:

> 'I advise them to try to publish at least one good thing in a good place before they hit the market. Yeah – and ideally two and possibly three. . . . I wish that weren't the case – but I think it would be – you know – a dereliction of duty not to encourage them in that way.'

This is the case even though many senior scholars know and openly talk about the fact that holding back one's work – improving and advancing it for a stronger and more developed publication in a few years' time – is almost always beneficial for the content. The thesis-turned-monograph published too early will be weaker for both scholar and discourse. And yet, the job market demands formal authorship early on.

This is a distancing of scholar and text. It is illuminating to witness that the competition arising out of this precedes intellectual development. It reifies early in scholarly careers the fact that something needs to get published, and only in a second instance is the question considered as to what is actually to be published, as a senior professor remarked. Early-career scholars are systemically discouraged from focussing on intellectual development so long as this stands in the way of constructing a record of formal authorship. To be sure, intellectual development can go hand in hand with the expansion of one's publication record. Engagement in discourse with one's early thinking may prove to be a fruitful endeavour even for this development. And yet, because the way publishing practices are constituted today with their inherent affectual mode of imperative, intellectual development may be prohibited more than it is supported. *Publish or perish* expresses this.

Publish or Perish Embodying Reification

Apart from referring to the terms of competition, *publish or perish* is also a narrative of their reification. This is embodied by the sayings and utterances of (non-scholarly) discourse about the requirement to compete with formal output. Such discourse indoctrinates these terms as unequivocal and indisputable. By engaging in discourse on *publish or perish*, early-career scholars reproduce the ideological construction of a rationalist solution to avert the uncertainty of uncertain futures in the sense of 'I only have to publish to avoid the death of my career'. This is not necessarily true, though; scholars may publish a lot but still not get the job.

The narrative construction comes about as a reflexive discourse with which individuals, especially early-career scholars, negotiate the insecurity of entering the academic job market. This discourse is reflexive in that scholars, by engaging in it, react to the increasing lengths of publication lists and their unknown own position in relation to others entering the job market, or to those with secure positions. This narrative is not: *to think or perish*, or: *to argue or perish*, or even: *teach or perish*. It is *publish or perish* since it is formal authorship that is said to count and, in turn, the illusionary idea that the *publication as output* indeed suffices as a way forward.

By engaging in such discourse, scholars not only contribute to the reification of its principles; early-career scholars also induce added pressure on themselves that potentially harms their intellectual development. As several both young and experienced scholars explain, those who claim to unplug themselves from this constant stream of comparison and conversing seem to deal better with the underlying alienation: they find ways of negotiating the pressure and their intellectual development by publishing less. Engagement in this discourse reproduces the identification of a solution that itself manifests the problem. It creates, as mentioned during my interviews, a *frantic dash* for publications that discourages alternatives.

This can also be seen in prominent self-help guides (for instance, Glatthorn, 2002; Harzing, 2016; Hills, 1987; Kelsky, 2015; Lussier, 2010; McNulty, 2013). They aim to help scholars become more productive in formalistic terms. They suggest that the way out of the precariat is paved by publications, since the practice of counting and comparing records of formal authorship is the most fundamental way of recognising productivity. In the end, they are symbolic of the *publish or perish* discourse and are, likewise, instances of the reification of its formal rationality.

Scholars always had to prove that they were better than or different from the crowd of competitors. But competition has grown more strenuous as the terms have been rationalised, moving (partially) away from exclusive circles but also reducing its substance to the appearance of a formal teleology. All the while, it cannot be claimed that long publication records are *always* demanded or that non-formally published works or pre-printed manuscripts submitted in a career application process are outright rejected. It is a symbolic narrative through which appearances of competition in material phenomena are mediated, so that scholars perceive that collectively reproduced practices are indeed appropriate.[15]

Moreover, no scholar has to engage in the discourse on *publish or perish* just as no one is forced to the *frantic dash* of relentless publishing. But it takes unconventional motivation not to reproduce established practice, that

---

[15] In the Bourdieusian sociology, this might be called the *illusio*. The *illusio* is the belief in a game and its righteousness, without substantive intelligibility of the working principles of this game, where a game is a bundle of practices geared towards a certain end (Bourdieu, 1998: 76). However, Bourdieu's diction categorically pronounces adverse structural effects such as a wilful internal competition, presenting collective meaning as a consistently negatively connoted 'collective adhesion to the game' (Bourdieu, 2006: 167). I do not believe that such intentional competition can be universally ascribed to scholars in the humanities.

is, motivation to resist the practice's immanent affect.[16] This motivation seems to be reserved for those who feel secure that their intellectual ability (or their network or institutional symbolism) suffices. This also plays a role in the working of the REF such that elite institutions allow their scholars more freedom to publish less and to focus on high-quality intellectual contributions.

The same seems to be true on a personal level where scholars' belief in their own ability fosters a strength to resist the negotiation of quantity and quality, and to take the time to focus on the latter. It is in this respect that such motivation is a matter of trust and good mentorship, a matter that most interviewees in my study see as quite risky. For most early-career scholars – faced with an uncertain future – it seems to be a high-risk strategy to disregard competition on formal authorship: who is there to judge and assure me that my few brilliant ideas (developed in unpublished manuscripts) will suffice? All strive to achieve more and, by looking at the best in their fields, aim to replicate such senior publication records. But how does an early-career scholar account for the instability of the first steps of scholarly thinking? Where to get the reassurance of the eminence of the slow process, of the few focussed publications? How can the early lecturer in the UK be sure of their position in the field if all around their publish frequently? Why put so much effort into this singular publication if quantity tends, or is said to tend, to be rewarded above quality? Others seem to be so versatile and adept as they contribute to this and that discourse, while I only have this one substantial piece, unpublished in the drawer of my desk. And, in the end, why put so much effort into a single publication if the single publication is hardly ever accorded the attention it may deserve? In other words, as a philosopher remarked during an interview after being asked why he publishes his scholarship: '[T]hat's a good question since it's not being read.'

Aspiring scholars rely on the production of formal authorship. Its yield appears to securely lead to job prospects and, thus, to an existence as a philosopher or historian, or at least a job. In this respect, formal authorship is a disciplining mode. One's own intellectual development and a thorough scholarly agenda stand in the shadow of a formal track of

---

[16] Routinised practices are seen as having immanent affect that compels actors to act in a certain way. Thus, affect can be seen as a motivational force in theory.

productivity. This is essentially Weberian formal rationality (Weber, [1922] 1978: 85). Since no normative frame to evaluate the ends of practices is in place, formal rationality places mere discipline above responsibility: one need only work hard enough in accordance with given (thin) ends – effectively working through means, that is, ticking boxes – until achievement rewards discipline.

Where the rationale of ticking boxes creates anxiety in its narrative representation of *publish or perish*, it also creates the false assurance that a way forward is possible on transparent, albeit strenuous terms. It advocates that an intellectual career can become plannable and manageable where insecurity and precarious employment suggest the opposite. It is the scholars outside of elite institutions – from minority or working-class backgrounds in particular – who are the most affected by this ambiguous setting. It increasingly extends to advanced levels of careers in the UK. As the data show, this is different in Germany where pressure rests much more on early-career positions and decreases steadily. The early insecurity of careers is even more intense in Germany than it is in the UK, as a recent, nationwide outcry of indignation again highlights (Bahr et al., 2021). This really focusses on the *early* stages of a career, diminishing the diversity of voices already at the entrance.

Moreover, this is a gender issue, too, across the two countries. The academic precariat of young scholars is known for being a hostile environment for planning and starting a family or raising children. A gender gap is reported in various instances where, by historical default, women are disadvantaged. Witness the different ways women are structurally underrepresented in the bibliometrics of authorship (Bendels et al., 2018; West et al., 2013). Such structural effects – arguably worse in the fields of science, technology, engineering, and mathematics than in the humanities but nonetheless so here – also prevail in many practices in academia such as hiring, promotion, and grant peer review (Bornmann et al., 2007; Larivière et al., 2013; Laufenberg et al., 2018; Moss-Racusin et al., 2012; van Dijk et al., 2014; Weisshaar, 2017). Ultimately, underrepresentation of female scholars in high-impact publications is even worse than it is for their underrepresentation in a scholarly discipline, as has been observed for the field of sociology (Akbaritabar and Squazzoni, 2020). My data also show that pressure to publish tends to be perceived as higher among women (Figure 33).

The connection of measurable output and career development for young women becomes blatantly clear where the sheer disciplinary workload of carving out publications stands against the tasks of raising children, where society still relies on traditional roles. Such work continues to miss the due recognition as a fundamental achievement, as the enduring debate showcases (Honneth, 2003: 141). The anecdotal evidence persists of women deciding to raise a child and, so, missing out on achieving a publication record that is as long as that of a male competitor who therefore gets the job. The 2020 lockdown in response to Covid-19 was evidence in this respect: the gender balance in journal submissions shifted towards male scholars and researchers, indicating that female scholars and scientists had other tasks to look after (Flaherty, 2020; Rusconi et al., 2020) – for society and hence also for academia, these are likely more important tasks than producing output, though they miss their due recognition.

4 Being REFable: The UK's REF and Germany's Traditionalism

Scholars in the UK have to become *REFable*. The REF is an epitome manifestation of the instrumentalisation of publishing in the UK. Its historical development has substantially influenced the grounds and ways of publishing. All the while, research management has taken over its principles so that these shifted grounds and ways are no longer tied to the REF itself. Particularly *the job market* – the way scholarly work is recognised and rewarded – is extending the influence of the historical impact of the REF. Being *REFable* is shorthand for the requirement of being fit for the scholarly job market based on authorship. Both quantitative and qualitative data substantiate the matter of *REFability* and provide further insights into the ways quantity, quality, and the temporal issues of *REFability* are – seemingly naturally – negotiated through publishing.

The chapter picks up several aspects discussed in the preceding chapters such as the value of marketable output, *publish or perish* as a reifying discourse, and the clustered distribution of experienced pressure. Preceding this discussion is a historical overview of the REF and the *Exzellenzinitiative*, followed by a closer look at the empirical situation of publishing practices and a discussion of how this is to be interpreted in a larger context.

A Short History of the REF

There are many aspects for which the REF – and the earlier Research Assessment Exercise (RAE) – is criticised: the way it reproduces existing hierarchies (Dix, 2016; Münch, 2008: 134); the mechanism of redefining institutional roles or moving efforts away from teaching (Frank et al., 2019; Henkel, 1999); the way it promotes competition but without fully considering corresponding market mechanisms (Frank et al., 2019; Shackleton and Booth, 2015); the fact that it is quite an expensive publicly funded exercise benefiting only a few institutions (Arnold et al., 2018); (resulting from this, it can be argued to be a classic example of an institution that is only giving the appearance of rational conduct while being primarily inefficient; see: Meyer and Rowan, 1977); the results of the

REF being transmuted from a funding into a 'research *ranking* system' (Brink, 2018: 82; emphasis in original) and its being partly based on an instrumentalist principle of benefit (Brink, 2018: 168–77); the costs of impact assessment of this mode being likely to outweigh its benefits (Martin, 2011); and the way it puts pressure particularly on younger scholars (Archer, 2008). Ultimately, as Frank et al. (2019: 81) call it, 'the RAE/REF became a victim of its own success', which means that it has acquired such a strong position that it has become a distortion of that which it was supposed to measure. In other words, the REF has fallen prey to Goodhart's law.

The REF's origin lies in cuts to grant funding and a new mode of strategic planning that came along with it. This was the task of the University Grants Committee (UGC) from 1983 onwards. The UGC was responsible for the distribution of core funding for research and teaching. This task was quite straightforward then, since universities in the UK were less hierarchically organised compared with, for instance, German universities. Researchers enjoyed a high degree of autonomy and flexibility with regard to research endeavours. Most funding was distributed based on unit size, with a few elite lobbying exceptions such as Oxford and Cambridge (Whitley et al., 2010: 53–4). During the Thatcher government, public spending was to be cut, which meant considerable reductions to funding. It was the UGC's task to determine a process to allocate reductions systematically. In hindsight, Swinnerton-Dyer, then chair of UGC, claims the key issue in this allocation was transparency (Jump, 2013). In other words, the question of which institution received cuts on what basis needed to be made clear to all involved. Alongside this, however, demands for more accountability rose as well. Future funds were to be distributed on the basis of clear and competitive objectives, efficient management, and measurable results. This already highlights key principles of the politics underlying the rising neoliberalism in these times more generally. As a result, the Research Selectivity Exercise (RSE) was initiated in 1986, often regarded as the first RAE despite its name variant.

The exercise's methodology was much simpler compared with today's REF, since the UGC itself ran on tight budgets. The RSE consisted of a questionnaire distributed to all units of assessment, which could be formed of individual departments, groups of departments, or parts of a department at a university and, therefore, varied considerably in size. The questionnaire enquired about matters such as 'research income, research planning, and priorities' as well as the unit's 'five best publications from the previous five years' (Whitley et al., 2010: 55). At this initial stage, the performance-based funding had little material influence. Nevertheless, complaints about a biased approach were voiced even during this earlier simple exercise (Jump, 2013). Likewise, the development towards managing research more professionally is visible already at this early stage, as 'the authority of university management vis-à-vis its researchers increased' (Whitley et al., 2010: 55). Backed by this development, the Universities Funding Council (UFC) replaced the UGC in 1988 and conducted a more sophisticated RSE in 1989 with a special focus on publication data, including relative output numbers and connections to full-time staff. This funding mechanism was dominated by the focus on publications and publicly visible outputs, which were to be peer reviewed. Units were subsequently rated, so that this second RSE already shows considerable similarities to the next funding round, then termed RAE, and to the later established REF.

In between the first RAE in 1992 and 1989's RSE, however, an important development took place: the 1992 Further and Higher Education Act ended the binary divide between universities and polytechnics.[17] This seemed to considerably increase competition for limited funds. It did so only formally, though. As Bence and Oppenheim show, depending on the 2,800 submissions from 192 institutions, 'older universities received 91% of available research funding, new universities 7% and colleges 2%' (Bence and Oppenheim, 2005: 146). This shows that the earlier voiced concerns over

---

[17] This is an important difference in comparison with Germany: such a binary divide still exists in Germany between *Universitäten* and *Fachhochschulen*. The latter do not offer humanities disciplines; earlier polytechnics in the UK often do so today, but they are often less research-intensive than traditional universities. See in this respect also Mandler's clarification that the massification of education in the UK 'meant proportionately less STEM [science, technology, engineering, and mathematics]' (Mandler, 2020: 178).

bias extended even beyond substantial reforms. From this point onwards, and even though this was initially conceived of as a mechanism for determining research funding in the context of cuts, the UK established for itself the basis of a performance-based research funding system (PRFS) which distributed funds on a competitive basis, until the present day's REF.

Today's REF between Symbolic and Material Reward

In its own words, today's REF 'is the UK's system for assessing the quality of research in UK higher education institutions' (REF, 2020a: n.p.). Its threefold purpose is to provide 'accountability for public investment', allow for a 'benchmarking' of the research conducted in the UK, and 'inform the selective allocation of funding' (REF, 2020b: n.p.). To fulfil such expectations, the funding bodies responsible for the REF conduct an extensive process of expert review of publication outputs and impact statements every four to six years. All potential fields of scholarly enquiry are divided into four main panels, in 2021 comprising a total of thirty-four units of assessment; panel D is the relevant section for arts and humanities.

In material terms, the REF is a mechanism of elite reproduction. Rather than distribution in effective terms – or even *re*distribution allowing for future potential – the REF seems to be just big enough to claim a position as a major funding mechanism and, all the while, small enough to concentrate on the historical elite and quickly fade out on a short tail of good, but not quite world-leading units. This concentration as reproduction of hierarchy is built into the exercise, just as 'over 50% of total QR [quality-related] funding [is] going to the top 10 universities' (Arnold et al., 2018: ii; see also Dean, 2018). Much more than the management of performance, this is the management of Weberian social closure.

And yet – or because of this – the REF must be seen as a mechanism for distributing symbolic much more than material reward: it is 'prestige rather than financial incentives as the main mechanism through which PRFSs work' (Hicks, 2012: 258). It is in this sense that the REF is a ritual manifestation of governance principles often referred to as NPM. Indirect coercion through the allure of exoteric rhetoric is the means of manageability much more than it is direct management of esoteric discourse. This shift from material gains to symbolic reward needs to be put into perspective as it fundamentally alters the way the REF is to be seen: it enforces the paradigm of consumerist education and marketable excellence generally, not just for those materially rewarded. It is not a necessity to gain funding; it is a necessity to gain, in some form, a marketable label as being better in relative terms.

Naively put, this is a paradox: the REF does not aspire to significantly substantiate beyond the elite (by means of funding) and, yet, it substantiates pervasively (the rhetoric of *the REF* is everywhere). This is the case because 'as a government-backed kitemark, a REF rating provides signals that are useful to universities from a marketing perspective' (Shackleton and Booth, 2015: 1). This – the marketing perspective in a consumerist appeal to education and scholarship – is the primary motivation for universities and their departments and institutes to care about the REF. It empowers universities to shift budgets towards performing better and advertising this performance, which requires managing recruitment and individual performativity in a way that allows for symbolic gains that can further enable potential for future recruitment and performativity. This indicates that it might be, rather, not a paradox but political intention. A former provost at UCL summarises this as he claims that a good REF outcome 'is a powerful way of enhancing reputation from which other benefits flow, such as recruitment of students and staff' (Lipsett, 2007: n.p.).

It is for this reason that the impact of the REF is experienced far beyond its material structures or direct influence. That is, even though it recurs only every few years, the efficient auditing of which it is a manifestation affects practices beyond the direct influence of the exercise in praxis. It is also for this reason that scholars see the impact of the REF actually in the – mythical reference to the – job market. Institutions mediate efficient auditing and principles of NPM in accordance with updates of the REF policy – they do not simply pass on the policy in their own guidelines of recruitment and promotions.

From Humboldt to the Exzellenzinitiative

I turn to Germany for comparison. The funding structures of German academia are quite different compared with those in the UK. One may claim that the humanities as an intellectual institution is the one academic resort in Germany that is the least touched by NPM. However, this is changing quickly. Today's humanities scholars in Germany are best characterised by a form of hybridity: they are rooted in a historical notion of humanities scholarship but, all the while, need to conform to new governance principles.[18]

Since the Humboldtian university reform and the dominance of bourgeois educational elites, the German *Geisteswissenschaften* have been a resort of the *Gelehrter* – the learned burgher, the erudite, even highbrow, socially sophisticated academic (Hamann, 2009: 42; Münch, 2007: 170; Münch, 2008: 166). Weber explicates this also as he renounces democratic access and refers to the *aristocracy of the mind* in German academia (Weber, [1917] 2015: 10). The Humboldtian ideal of real scholarship as an education that forms character in respect to national (Prussian) interests similarly needs to be remembered (Humboldt, [1810] 2017: 155). This ideal centred on the individual within a particular societal and cultural setting. It resulted from the construction of a scholar subject that dominated the intellectual elite in Germany as well as continental Europe more generally. Where the UK's humanities have originally been stratified into elite and non-elite, Germany's *Geisteswissenschaften* are rooted in a homogeneity of scholarliness that defines itself through its traditional ideals. Historically, the ivory tower was coherently inhabited by all humanities scholars – with professorship – in Germany; they were the *Gelehrte* as the elite, unconcerned with practical matters and above the plebeian masses. In the UK, this was true only for a smaller circle within elite institutions alongside a heterogeneity of institutions serving more worldly ideals of education for private sector careers. Practices of communication embodied this ideal in their mode of circulating ideas among those involved. This resembles in some ways the authorial professor, equipped with so-called

---

[18] Reckwitz exemplifies hybridity in his sociology of culture as a matter of subjectification: different culture logics are superimposed upon each other, making for an imbrication of potentially contradictory principles; they construct a canvas of instability and frictions which shape the developments of subjects. Earlier cultures or subject formations mark cultural differences – *constitutive outsides* in the terminology of Reckwitz (2020: 98) – which represent dismissed or abandoned principles within itself from which, all the while, the modern subject still draws positively.

cultural capital by their institution, as explicated by Bourdieu (1988: 36) for the academic field in France.

The impinging impact of NPM and efficient auditing arrived only recently in Germany. Its bearing is felt only more harshly where its formal rationalistic terms increasingly tie practices to formal managerialism. In response, the ideal-type values of humanistic scholarship abate to exert power. Just as a hybridity suggests, logics of traditionalism persist for some practices while new governance changes practices only partially. There are more and more critics now who claim that NPM has already taken over the institution that the humanities in Germany once claimed. It enforces a thinning of ends as it replaces the Bourdieuian *Homo Academicus* with an *Homo Oeconomicus*. Output has to be *managed* today where contribution was *judged* in previous times. In the language of Liessmann (2006: 39), this is the turning from knowing in terms of a humanistic ideal to the industrialisation of knowledge. The German humanities faculty is a mass institution today that is, nevertheless, still governed by the power of a few. Particularly within this power – in both discourse and professorial representation – traditionalisms remain.

The *Exzellenzinitiative* is a manifestation of this new hybridity; a new research governance in opposition to traditional scholarly power. It is at once similar to the REF and particularly German. Materially, the *Exzellenzinitiative* is also an elite funding mechanism. Other than the REF, however, the *Exzellenzinitiative* does not practise the management and symbolic reward of output generally. It mechanistically enforces Germany's goal to become an internationally more visible and esteemed base for research and scholarship. The result is similar to the REF in an international perspective: advertise the national position of excellence to attract students and scholars. But the means is different: the *Exzellenzinitiative* is much less connected to managed output.

The idea of the *Exzellenzinitiative* began with a paper on innovation strategy published by the German Social Democrats in 2004; it claimed that Germany needed elite universities of international standing (Sondermann et al., 2008: 10). Despite criticism of the nature of elite funding, it was rapidly taken up in political and public discourse and the idea developed into a full-fledged strategy to incentivise new monopoly structures within the traditional homogeneity of German universities (Münch, 2007: 47). The official strategy was released in 2005. Its method was initially connected to project funding. The institution-wide award was subsequently geared to the establishment of such funded projects. Universities applied in two competitive rounds for this distinct funding (580 applications in total with 85 funded projects/centres; Sondermann et al., 2008: 11). It was awarded on the basis of peer review – of projects, not of publications – with internationally renowned scholars.

Subsequently, nine universities were awarded the status of *Exzellenzuniversitäten*. Thirty-seven universities were funded in the first round, but only nine universities got the institutional award of the *Exzellenzuniversität* (and only 2.3 per cent of the overall funding was awarded to universities in the former East Germany, meaning that concerns of biased approaches were raised in Germany, too; Pasternack, 2008: 20). This highlights the double-edged aim of this politics: the awarding procedure led to the establishment of a core elite as well as the break-up of the homogeneous university structure more broadly. The establishment of graduate schools – a highly criticised institutional type very unlike the traditional German university – got broad uptake and universities prepared for future funding rounds of this kind beyond the target of the *Exzellenz* status. Similar to the REF, though, the strong focus on research and excellence led to a decreasing focus on teaching and to processes of monopolisation of higher education resources by fewer institutions (Pasternack, 2008: 23), as well as to a material reorientation of institutions towards targets that arise from without scholarly practices (Münch, 2011: 18).

This political strategy breaks with the Humboldtian ideal of the German university and especially with the historical denotation of the German *Gelehrter*. It manifests new governance principles that aim to break with the – often praised – homogeneity of German universities by encouraging the construction of excellence. German universities are to be stratified into elite and non-elite as is the case in anglophone countries (Wohlrabe et al., 2019: 20). Such funding approaches have the clear objective of 'improving the international competitiveness' (Schroder et al., 2014: 224). Where the grounds of competition shift towards the construction of reputation external to discourse, the terms on which scholars are to compete likewise shift from scholarly substance to external management. The need to internationalise scholarly output to establish worldwide authorship visibility as a matter of excellence is a chimera in regard to scholarly substance; it resembles principles of NPM per se. This outsources the notion of quality, taking it from the realms of discourse to those of governance, which ushers in a logic of mistrust and where the means to determine productivity become an end on their own (Münch, 2011: 113), one that is irrespective of the actual development of scholarly discourse. However, its impact is much less concerned with the subjectification of the German scholar in the context of publishing practices. On the one hand, it seems to focus – for now – on the few institutions that actually intend to compete (only forty-one universities officially applied in the latest round; thirty-four of those have been awarded the funding of fifty-seven projects; DFG, 2018). On the other hand, the initiative is also much less focussed on the publication histories of the individuals within an institution; instead, it rewards future concepts of combined projects. This is a decisive difference in the context of the REF.

Nevertheless, its scholarly awkward marketing logic is the same. Based on the latest round (then renamed *Exzellenzstrategie*), there are eleven official *Exzellenzuniversitäten* in Germany, which will receive added funding of about €13 million each per year for seven years (Warnecke, 2019). The universities of Göttingen and Freiburg are not part of this circle, but they were *Exzellenzuniversitäten* in earlier rounds. These institutions are renowned for their scholarship and their long history of praised thinkers in the humanities. One may refer to them as excellent institutions, but you are not allowed to call them *Exzellenzuniversität* for now. The substance has to bow before the formal identification in this instance, too. I now turn to its manifestation in the context of publishing.

Being REFable: Individuals and the Pressure to Perform

The empirical situation of experienced pressure in relation to the official assessments becomes visible in my data, both quantitatively and qualitatively. Figures 45 and 46 show that only a little impact is being perceived by German scholars in this regard. However, impact reaches soaring rates in the UK and is predominantly negative. Even after twenty-five years in academia, half of all UK scholars in the humanities experience a negative impact. The rate of negative impact reaches nearly 80 per cent among those experiencing high pressure to publish.

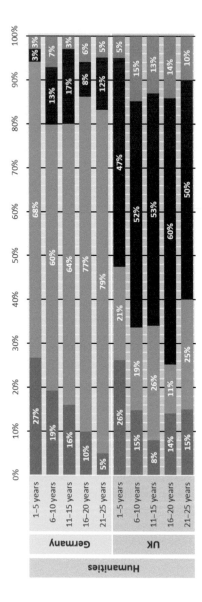

Figure 45 Publication behaviour affected by research assessments.

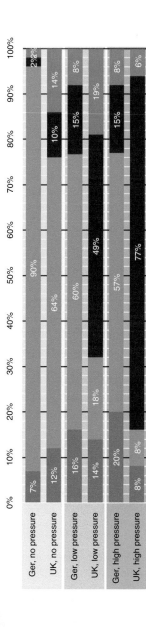

Figure 46 Publication behaviour affected by research assessments, in pressure clusters.

Moreover, scholars in the UK experience soaring levels of pressure to publish faster in relation to assessments, as can be seen in Figures 47 and 48. German scholars rather reject this form of pressure. This pressure is aggravated in the UK and reaches nearly 90 per cent among those experiencing high pressure generally. Again, it remains high long into the career.

The strong connection to official assessments in the UK, the perceived temporal pressure, and its relation to quality all substantiate that authorship and publishing are practices through which a systemic pressure to perform is funnelled. The differences of distributions among early-career scholars between the two countries reiterate the different competitive relations and their terms. The REF is dominantly connected to negative pressure in the UK. German scholars reject such a perceived impact of assessments on publishing. The relative impact, represented in pressure clusters, is instructive in terms of the distribution, especially in the UK. There is a near eightfold increase of a perceived connection between those who experience no pressure and those experiencing high pressure. This means that the negative impact of the REF on a scholar's publishing is experienced as being tremendously stronger if they indicate experiencing publishing pressure generally – or that this general pressure really is an effect of the REF. The share of scholars indicating a positive connection more than halves between the two groups (Figure 46).

The dominance of official assessments over publishing practices can be seen already in this quantitative information. The negative impact indicated here is a key explanation for the instrumentalisation of publishing in the UK. Issues such as temporality and perceived quality help clarify the mode of its impact. Though a fraction of scholars seem to experience temporal pressure positively, the overwhelming number of scholars who confirm the prevalence of temporal pressure indicate a negative impact. The same is true in respect of quality; though there are some scholars who indicate perceived temporal pressure alongside less of an impact on the quality of their work, most scholars claim that this temporal pressure indeed leads to the quality of their work suffering.

Since a concern with publishing in regard to research assessments is much less of an issue in Germany, the connections with temporality and impact on quality also have to be read differently. It has to be borne in mind,

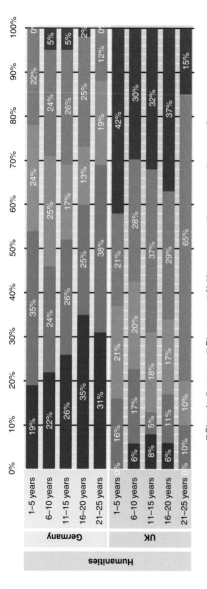

Figure 47 Pressure to publish faster in relation to research assessments ('I feel pressured to publish faster so that the publications can be included in research assessments (the REF / Exzellenzinitiative)').

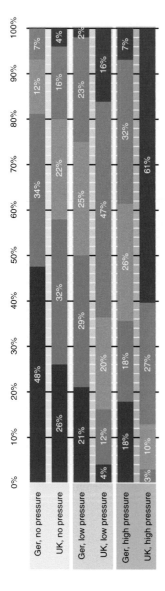

Figure 48 Pressure to publish faster in relation to research assessments ('I feel pressured to publish faster so that the publications can be included in research assessments (the REF/ Exzellenzinitiative)'), in pressure clusters.

most of all, that even among scholars who claim to experience a high amount of pressure to publish, merely one among six scholars claims that research assessments play a negative role in this respect (it is four out of five scholars in the UK). This difference from the UK is also visible in detail where the issue of temporality and perceived quality has the opposite appearance in Germany. Only a few scholars claim that they perceive a pressure to publish earlier in order to have their publications included in research assessments. All the while, many more scholars perceive a temporal pressure generally, which they see as having an impact on the quality of their publications.

It can be inferred, therefore, that temporality does have an impact in Germany, although it is much smaller than in the UK. Most of all, it is not connected to a recurring assessment procedure but to the need to perform on formal output early in a career (as especially the more tenure-track path of the *Juniorprofessor* demands). Thus, the *Exzellenzinitiative*, unlike the REF, cannot be seen as a material source of pressure, even though pressures are abstractly funnelled by that which is often called *the job market*.

These data can be contextualised with insights from the qualitative interviews. Positive voices were scarce during my interviews, aligning with the impression provided by the quantitative data. If something positive is remarked about the REF, it is the assumption that the REF at least tries to be a scholarly endeavour since it builds on a form of peer review. There seems to be a sense of scholarly accountability in that scholars are mutually respectful while reviewing each other's work since, in the end, they are all in the same boat. Another beneficial effect of the REF is said to be the way it can push senior colleagues to publish who would otherwise not publish (though they may be teaching, nevertheless).

Other than that, voices are frustrated or even angry. The REF is positioned as a powerful mechanism shaping publishing pressures. It does this in different ways. While the negotiating of quantity and quality (as discussed in Chapter 3) is an issue rather for early-career scholars, scholars more experienced in their careers need to balance quality much more with temporality. Quantity is a key issue for strategising publishing to appear performatively well positioned early on. The production of high amounts of output is the way out of the precariat in both Germany and the UK. The strategising of publications does not end after these early-career positions in the UK, though. The scholar has to remain *REFable*.

Even senior academics put the REF forward as a primary reason to publish and to do so today, rather than tomorrow, or to produce another article rather than focussing on a monograph (though this is less the case at elite institutions). This also encompasses practical concerns: contributions to edited collections are not worth as much for the institutional career, and some publishers take years to publish such a volume. Even though the REF does not suggest a genre formally, it does so practically.

Discourse is, thus, shaped by comprising *REFable* output. This output is not driven from within discourse, despite claims that the REF is regarded by some as a scholarly exercise (because of its peer review). Scholars exemplify in diverse ways how authorship is alienated or how guidelines and rhetoric push a sense of conformism. And the alienation is experienced even more broadly, as a senior philologist explained to me: '[T]here is such hostility and there is so much authority vested in the REF – it gives a license to bully academics who do not follow the rules – who don't go along with the crowd.'

Scholars experience pressure to conform to institutional guidelines or the everyday discourse about performance. For some scholars – especially senior scholars with permanent positions or those who have a strong record of, or current ability to develop, scholarship – this pressure may mean choosing one publisher instead of another for a monograph because of its time to publication. It may also mean, simply, finally finishing an article, a positive encouragement to finish work that is likely to be of solid quality. Seniors and the high achievers, so to say, are more or less pressured in regard to the ways they publish. This is different for the (yet) less-secure and less-well-positioned scholars.

The differential impact of the REF showcases how wider principles are at play, rather than a direct, material coercion of the REF. Individual scholars often do not know explicitly about the official policy. They rather know (bits of) the requirements put forward by their departments, or indeed only floor chatter. In this sense, the rhetoric is all about the REF, but it is more the mythical invisible hand of *the job market* that has taken over its principles. It is, in the end, an individual's desire to stay in the career or get promotion that reinforces the seemingly rationalistic solution in praxis. It is an issue that many scholars have constantly in mind, especially as mock exercises make the looming task repeatedly more obvious.

For the same reason, the impact of quantity is still there, although it is a historical relict. Quantity is bounded in today's REF. Earlier in the RAE, however, it was a mode of *the more, the better*. As senior scholars explain, this management of quantity continues as a residue in the minds of research managers and, as some scholars say, also in the minds of young scholars. This feeds into the narrative of *publish or perish*. This historical impact of the REF connects to the earlier discussion of intellectual development and *unplugging* from the discourse on *publish or perish*. Because of this – partly peer-induced – pressure, scholars publish too quickly or too early. However, looking at the intense competition on the early-career job market and its seemingly borderless expanse, it indeed seems a risk to appear intellectually highly developed but non-performative in terms of author-ship; it is a risk to develop your philosophy if it does not result in publications that fit into existing discourses.

Moreover, since REF guidelines – the way official requirements trans-late into individual demands – vary by institution, the immediate pressure also varies; this variation is often abstractly attributed to the notion of the job market. An experienced philosopher summarises this as follows: '[A]t the moment the immediate pressure is coming from the universities themselves more than directly through the REF.' Correspondingly, scho-lars from high-impact institutions are often allowed more freedom. Institutional and departmental guidelines are less strict at these institu-tions as the scholars are trusted to produce valuable publications in time; it is a trust building on the social closure that is already in place at the initial granting of positions. Non-high-impact institutions gear their scholarly employees towards stricter guidelines, using the REF to urge them to publish.

The REF is, in this sense, reinforcing social closure among individual, young scholars. If their intellectual ability allows them to get a job at an elite institution, they experience less of the pressure of formal output and can focus on their intellectual development, which may set the grounds for the future few but high-quality publications. It is likely, therefore, that competing on formal output is even less of a concern for scholars at renowned institutions, whose futures are already less uncertain because of their potentially stronger networks and reputable institutional names. In this sense of social closure, 'PRFSs encourage excellence at the expense of equity' (Hicks, 2012: 259). A mechanism that is supposed to feature a few as a form of fostering and promoting an elite affects the whole negatively.

The result of this exercise is similar to making sure that only the cream of a cake is visible, while the rest of the cake – indeed, whole other cakes – stay invisible. This cream, termed excellence, comes about in labelled statements, representing scholarship that is of '[q]uality that is world-leading in terms of originality, significance and rigour' (REF, 2014: 60). While this may sound like an exercise that honours merit above all else, this applied insinuation of meritocracy is an illusion – just as the idea of meritocracy ever was. This illusion suggests that the REF is an exercise about the effective (re)distribution of funds based on historical performance. Primarily, however, the REF is about reputation. Performance is constructed to be most representative in terms of reputation within the existing stratification of universities who achieve the most performative output. As research management at less visible institutions aims to achieve some form of performative visibility, too, scholars there have to rush to produce more and more output. With a high amount of output, the reasoning might be, the chances of high impact are higher.

This pressure – ascribed to the REF but translated to practice by research management – on developing and mid-level scholars is about the construction of a scholarly artificial value much more than it is about creating a meaningful scholarly identity. Those two can coincide, of course, but the rhetoric and hiring practices suggest that the development of identity increasingly matters less. This is what Collini refers to as he writes that because of mere bibliographic measurement, younger scholars will be discouraged from conducting major projects that do not lead to continuous output but that are, if completed, 'worth far more than a whole CVful of slight articles and premature "syntheses"' (Collini, 2012: 127). Such mechanisms can have a devastating impact on the development and meaning of identity and notions of scholarly meaningfulness. Scholarly work needs to be valuable in terms that are marketable to the institution today. In the wake of this governance, the '"successful", authentic academic identities are rendered insecure, temporary and risky within regimes of performativity' (Archer, 2008: 392). Intellectual authenticity and identity are desirable by institutions only as long as they do not prohibit constant output as measurable performance.

REFable is, therefore, a euphemism for performance that is primarily formally measurable. And these shifts are expanding to senior scholars where 'staff perceived as underperforming on research would be moved to teaching contracts' (Baker, 2020a; see also Baker, 2020b). Moreover, universities increased early retirement inducements resulting from a strategy 'seen by some as a sign of institutions shedding academics who they perceived to be underperforming' on the way towards the next REF (Grove, 2020). Beware: your world-leading performance will only be remembered until the next REF cycle.

The Management of Internationalisation and Impact

Talking to scholars about publishing in relation to the REF during my interviews has a very mechanistic, instrumental appeal. The focus seems to be all about output. The sense of alienation is evident throughout the conversations. The REF contributes to the distancing of scholar and text. A summary of it, as stated before, is: the REF does not review past discourse as it was shaped from within – discourse is shaped from without to be reviewed by a future REF.

The sphere referred to as *the job market* is the discursive sphere in which requirements and experiences are negotiated, manifesting rhetoric and exhibiting the governance principles that suggest that formal output is more valuable than the underlying scholarship. The material manifestation is only one instance that merges with rhetoric and manifold guises of discourse to emerge in the form in which it is experienced. As several interviewees explicate, you could do away with the REF today and not much would change in praxis. The REF's principles go far beyond its material guidelines as these are embodied by the way scholarly work is being valued and rewarded today. This suggests that the meaning of scholarly labour is perceived not in the intrinsic substance of scholarly discourse but as instrumental means. In this respect, the REF is a *good* way to increase a nation's visibility and reputation in terms of excellence and contributing to supranational elites – *good* as in: instrumentally effective. This, however, is not necessarily based on – and certainly does not improve – scholarly merit in its intrinsic sense. It is essential to point out explicitly that this rhetoric and the distribution of labels of excellence do not pertain to scholarly communities. The notion of the job market exhibits the different guises this can have – in the mode of negotiating quantity or quality, temporality or genre, institutional guideline or informal chatter. Output is the target to which scholarship has to conform.

Impact case studies further exhibit the focus on output enforced by the REF. Impact is defined 'as an effect on, change or benefit to the economy, society, culture, public policy or services, health, the environment or quality of life, beyond academia' (REF, 2020c: 90). Though this can be specified in more detail for relevant areas, the fact remains that there is an underlying assumption of instrumentalism. These studies 'signal the continuing neoliberalisation of higher education' as well as the 'commodification of seemingly every facet of academic life' (Watermeyer and Hedgecoe, 2016: 663). They build upon a systemic neglect of the consideration and judgement of whether and how impact is desirable in the humanities. The idea seems to be that scholarship that is innovative and efficiently externalised is more beneficial than anything else – any other form of advancement of discourse and any other form of voice. It is a neglect of the way scholarship impacts on the people – students, avid readers, fellow scholars – who partake in practices of society and, thus, turns esoteric discourse by means of their personality and identity into culturally desirable, principled human conduct without manipulative detour. Efficiently externalised means that teaching is inferior to narrated cases of external impact. For sure, teaching *can* be submitted for the REF. But it requires 'corroborating evidence for impact case studies' (REF, 2020c: 13), such that teaching needs to be put into an eventful, narrative context where mere notions of learning and debating do not suffice. Dialogue is a distraction.

If we consider Germany, the impact is divided. As discussed, publishing is not affected by such procedures as much as in the UK. Nevertheless, academia is caught in a hybridity of traditionalism and progress – in the being of the *Gelehrte* and the governance of NPM. Formal proceduralism persists from earlier times next to a new governmentality so that publishing practices are bound to both historically grown principles and new progressive terms of excellence and internationality. This results in subtler, semantically contradictory, but nonetheless systemic forms of an instrumentalisation of publishing. Firstly, there is a race to catch up in Germany, a desire to be legitimated in an international *market of scholarly ideas*. To fit this market's terms, the publishing practices of German scholars have to adapt to an international context. While the German *Exzellenzinitiative* has almost no direct impact on authorship and publishing, it exemplifies rationalistic governance principles where excellence and efficiency are guiding terms without consideration of a local specificity of humanities scholarship. Secondly, formal authorship is a tool of bureaucratic accountability. To publish, in this sense, means to legitimate and fulfil requirements of funding. A conference is not finished without the publication of a *Sammelband*. In turn, discourses become crowded by unread accounts of conferences or, on terms of similar traditionalist logics, by qualifying scriptures such as PhD theses.

The matter of enforced internationalisation is particularly pertinent. Publishing practices become geared towards internationality as the publications are mediated by a governance that favours international output above regional specificity, irrespective of discourse. This insinuates a formalism where, indeed, internationality gains a symbolic value that can be measured without qualitative judgement of content. Remember here the data provided earlier about the use of secondary language in German humanities scholarship: English or a mix of English and German dominate. German scholars see in this a potentially disastrous tendency for their scholarship.[19] Internationality is not global inclusivity; neither is it specific to discourse. The drive towards English cannot be justified by means of reception or content. As Stekeler-Weithofer states, actual internationalisation becomes manifest through the *reception* of a *diversity* of languages, instead of through mere *publishing* of *English* as is currently evident (Stekeler-Weithofer, 2009:

---

[19] This *Westernisation* results in epistemic injustices as the debate about global OA shows (Knöchelmann, 2021b).

36), a statement that reiterates the humanistic ideal. Boehm repeats this very ideal for art history and bemoans the discipline's canonisation as anglophone discourse (Boehm, 2009: 62). It is manifest even in obituaries that '"internationality" is a more pressing imperative for academics in Germany than the US' (Hamann and Zimmer, 2017: 1427). Jehne reiterates the ideal for the discipline of history in Germany where the reception of different languages is still common, while the publishing practices, ideally, also tie language with the topic focus of scholarship. And yet, he recounts the telling story (Jehne, 2009: 60) that a funding body initiated the introduction of a rating but had to realise that the parameter *internationalisation* (in terms of a diversity of languages and geographies) would lead to the exclusion of most of the esteemed American journals – they often require English only. This made the impasse obvious that desired esteem not necessarily connects with the scholarly ideals rooted in diversity or regional specificity.

If increased citation rates, collaboration, and mobility of scholars are considered good measures of success, then internationality may indeed be a precondition of success of national academic fields (Aufderheide and Neizert, 2016). But are citation rates, crude collaboration, and mobility of scholars good measures in the humanities? Tools to increase productivity and internationalisation claim to foster collaboration and invite international scholars into a nation's academic institutions. This appears to be a favourable endeavour. And yet, an indifference to the intrinsic purposes of scholarship may mean a focus on such an endeavour without acknowledging the societal and cultural role the – to be internationalised – scholarship has regionally. In other words, what is cut off by enforcing internationalisation in every project? What remains if more and more contributions to discourse are forced to be contributions to a regionally unspecific discourse? Will this enforce, in one of my interviewee's terms, a *dereliction of language-specific discourse* – an abandonment of the humanistic ideal of different cultures and languages coexisting in the humanities?

Besides forced internationalisation, publishing practices are marked by a mode of formal proceduralism in Germany. Many publications seem to exist as archives instead of as communicative means as they are reformulations of conference material. The result is the release of published artefacts that pile up on library shelves without readership – those interested in the reception have usually already received the message during the respective projects or meetings. In the critical terminology of Münch (2008: 176), these masses of artefacts contribute little to discourse and cause a feeling of *over-satiation* among scholarly communities. Such *over-satiation* is well documented in my interviews as well. Likewise expressed in my interviews, and as Münch also asserts, is that submissions to the *Sammelbände* are often half-baked (Münch, 2011: 160; see also Fohrmann, 2009; Jehne, 2009). They have been discussed already at conferences and no one expects them to be read. Authorship is considered to be a means of accountability here. This reiterates the principle of formal output, though it is for the sake not of providing evidence for new knowledges but of formally fulfilling the requirements of funding.

Such mechanisms provide insights into the constitution of publishing practices in Germany and how the practices differ from those in the UK. They show that it is much less institutional pressure in the form of performative output of something new that affects publishing; rather, it is traditional logics *next to* the demands of a new governance. All the while, actualisations of NPM evoke a conflict with the traditional, deemed quasi-feudal hierarchies of the German *Lehrstühle* (professorial chairs) within German universities. It is this combination – tenured professors maintaining reputation and position, formal rationalistic terms of competition among the *Mittelbau* – that leads to the empirical situation that young scholars bear pressure induced by new governance while senior, tenured professors experience almost none. It is also for this reason that a proposed solution to the devastating employment situation in Germany is to replace the *Lehrstuhl* with a departmental structure that resembles that in the UK (Specht et al., 2017). This would spoil the eminence of the German professorship and put more power into the hands of the exploited *Mittelbau*. It is questionable, however, whether this would also usher in more demands of output (as is already visible with the *Juniorprofessor* throughout the data presented earlier). The strengthening of the individual in such new departmental structures would, therefore, have to go hand in hand with a different recognition and reward of scholarly work. Changing the career setting is one aspect; changing the way scholarly work is respected is another.

Looking more abstractly at assessment exercises, their peculiarity is that they are 'perverting a procedure ... which is inherent in modern science and scholarship anyway' (Liessmann, 2006: 100; translation by the author). Most of what the humanities originally have is discourse. It comes about in the form of oral dialogue or published artefacts in which scholars take on each other's work recursively. Evaluation constantly takes place *within* both these means in the form of engagement with and judgement of content. The very basis for the symbolic value of contributions and venues comes about via the discursive approval and appreciation *within* discourse. The social objectification that enables symbolic reward of venues is possible in the first place only as scholars interact with content from a venue's programme (even though this may be a historical relict). In other words, the value of scholarly work is most visible in the recursive structure of dialogue.

National politics of research management hardly take note of this. This is the primary mark of alienation resulting from them. The REF and the *Exzellenzinitiative* meet in their proposition to manage scholarship so that it fulfils a certain function. Principles of marketable impact, internationalisation, and measurable output are manifest in both countries. And yet, while the REF does so by means of publication output, Germany does so by means of future project proposals (that are partly tied to output). Thus, looking at the REF helps in understanding publishing practices much more than looking at the *Exzellenzinitiative*. The REF marks an elongation of the principles articulated by *publish or perish* such that scholars have to legitimate their productivity through formal authorship. In Germany, the impact is more differentiated: the imperative to internationalise effects a change of the ways to engage in discourse – even the question of which discourse to contribute to in the first place. The proceduralism of accountability, instead, can much less be understood in terms of individual pressure in relation to subsistence. It is a systemic mobilisation that slowly clogs the pipelines of reasonable communicative practice. In both cases, nonetheless, an enforcement of an alienated condition becomes manifest, legitimated by governance.

All this is reminiscent of the *Thatcherite nationalism* that Readings already lamented (Readings, 1999: chapter 3; see also Harvie, 2000: 109). It is a raising of awareness for a nationalist sense of performance irrespective of the cultural specifics of that region, its society and (sub-)cultures, so that consumers of *world-leading* education and scholarship find their ways to the excellence of the UK's institutions. Such Thatcherite nationalism becomes likewise visible in Germany – except that the denotation Thatcherite seems defective. Short governmental cycles may provide the keywords, but they are usually only name-giving references to larger political trends that they exemplify. In the case of excellence and internationalisation as mechanisms aiming to improve a nation's standing, Thatcherite, thus, denotes only the drivers of neoliberalism and its governmentality that are actualised in almost all institutions of society.

5 Publishing as Production and the Meaning of Authorship

What exactly is the point of publishing? Now that we have discussed the empirical reality of authorship and publishing in the three preceding chapters, can a comprehensive answer to this question be spelt out? I aim to do this in this last chapter. It will be both a conclusion to the data and the interviews and an abstraction from them in order to reach a more general understanding of the recognition of scholarly work in today's humanities departments.

This also connects the discussion of authorship and publishing with wider issues of the humanities, particularly the debate of their – assumed, suggested, or projected – normative purpose. Calls of a crisis of the humanities are ongoing alongside chases for potential solutions (Belfiore, 2013; Drees, 2021; Fish, 2008; Kagan, 2009; Marquard, 2020a; Small, 2013). To be sure, this book is by no means an answer to this debate. And yet, identification of the self-referential practice that authorship and publishing have become very well provides an argument for it. Its claim is to seek a different recognition of the work of scholars that, in turn, allows for new ways – or the strengthening of old ways – of integrating and positioning scholarship within society.

I first conclude the discussion of authorship and publishing with two shorter sections on the constitution of publishing and the resultant meaning of authorship. I then turn to the concept of the distancing of scholar and text, which aids understanding of the self-referentiality of publishing.

The Constitution of Publishing

A conclusion of the preceding chapters – and of my conversations with scholars in the humanities in particular – is that individual intellectual development and dialogical engagement with others are subordinate to the production of output. Appearing productive on time and being measurably visible are key for making a career as a scholar; scholarship has to accommodate the production of output. Intellectual development and dialogue cannot be counted, measured in terms of easy heuristics, or marketed in a global race to excellence. It is in this sense to be understood that publishing and authorship are geared more towards formal criteria of *marketable output* than to *contributing to discourse*.

This is already visible on an individual level in the semantics of answers to the question about motives to publish. The scholars I interviewed claim that they are paid to publish, that publishing is demanded for their career, that they are required to be visible, or that they must publish in order to get the next grant. Publishing practices are ways to negotiate and adapt to managerial formal requirements. The wish to communicate scholarship often appears only as a secondary, somewhat implicit reason. This hierarchy – first production of output, second engagement with discourse – is the summary of a systemic alienated condition in the sense of a distancing of scholar and text, a distancing of scholarship and the communicative purpose of textual resources. The result is scholars with CVs full of publications but no resources to engage with teaching purposes or the masses of publications out there, and masses of publications that receive neither the due attention of an audience nor the focus and care of a writer. These masses are the majority; the race to become visible only strengthens the heuristics that make visible the elite.

This is not to say that scholars universally do not engage purposefully with discourse. They still tend to be rooted in an intrinsic desire to know and share knowledge. Likewise, the accumulation of reward accounted for in text as output or in the reputation of venues is bounded by the reception of text. As long as the reception of text – its substance in discourse – plays a crucial role in the humanities, heuristics only work up to a degree. And as all interviewees agree, at a certain stage in the process of awarding a grant or promotion, some pieces of text are being read. In other words, reception still matters. It does so less and less, though. The terms for being able to become a scholar or for remaining in a paid position to further knowledge depend more and more on an efficiency that the awareness of text in individual reception cannot provide. This efficiency is the established praxis of a particular mode of governance. Its principle is that formal evidence of output is the existentialist precondition of being a scholar.

The result is not only a burden – an experienced pressure – on the individual. It affects scholarly collectives as well as society. Advancement of knowing and understanding what it means to be human is funnelled through formal output regimes. Understanding, cultural meaning-making, and hermeneutical competences appear in the form of pieces of information. Other forms of evidence of intellectual pursuits – of scholarly labour – decrease in value. Teaching and informal communication are sidelined by the publication as output that results in formal authorship. Deliberation and dialogue – the foundations of humanistic scholarly endeavour – are degraded to minor tasks. They are not marketable in official assessments as their elusiveness misses the definite form that comes with authorship and the concreteness of a product. Text in the manifestation of produced output can yield the mystical added value of an efficiently comparable product better than any other form of scholarship.

The *publication as output* is a belief in the righteousness of some forms of publications and their heuristics above others as well as in the position of *published research* above all else. It is a belief enforced by the seemingly rationalistic narrative of publish or perish. Publishing practices, in this sense, centre on the transformation of text into the *publication as output*. It is the practice of making thought – its elusiveness, complexity, and specificity – comparable and generalisable. It means making it an equivalent next to others in the form of a product that steps out of the complexity and specificity of discourse. Text becomes manageable in its relation to others of the same output class.

The Formal Form of Authorship

This mode of recognition of scholarly work adds ambiguity to the already ambivalent term *author*. The dualistic appreciation of the author – the one that readers evoke in discourse and the individual who writes – is sidelined by formal authorship. This is the authorship accounted for on the CV.

Among many other things, authorship can be understood as a function in discourse in a Foucauldian sense (Foucault, 1979); it can be a community-constructed social reference (Ramdarshan Bold, 2018); it may denote being 'entitled to some portion of the credit for writing the manuscript' (Borenstein and Shamoo, 2015: 268); it may be a point of reference in the construction of corpora of knowledge (Hyland, 1999); it can be a reference in a politicised linearity of names with indifference to contributions as is common in the *team sciences* (Falk-Krzesinski et al., 2011) of scientific disciplines (this politicisation and questionable contribution is exemplified by the discussion of what constitutes authorship in the sciences; see Franck, 1999; Hundley et al., 2013; Siegel, 2008). Also in the sciences, the author might be regarded as a storyteller, constructing the story of nature (Knöchelmann and Schendzielorz, 2023). Authorship can represent the complexity of writing practices and may simply be the name of a person on a publication, being a material denotation in terms of copyright, inventorship, or ideational ownership.

All these relations – clustered in regard to discourse and social subject – need to be borne in mind in debates about authorship. Authorship ambivalence and its reflexive effect cannot be cut out to favour either side of it; they are mutually dependent. Authorship denotes the complex of references both of intellectual contribution to its contributor *and* of material publication to the individual. The former refers to discourse or content, and a communicative intent or implication of text in reception; the latter refers to social interrelation since it implies material, political, and non-textual symbolic motives. The author of text contributes to discourse, advances it by differentiation, and gains symbolic meaning as an intellectual position; the author also identifies with an individual who gains material reward. This ambivalence continues into the minutiae of writing and referencing text. In all these relations, the modes of authorship are interdependent.

Formal authorship cuts through these layers and their interdependency. It stands outside of discourse – it precedes it. Nevertheless, it is this form of authorship that fares as a key resource in the recognition and governance of scholarly work. The pervasive focus on output production is a reduction of the layered complex of discursive author and writer. Text no longer primarily communicates; it is a product that refers to its producer, to be located within a peer-reviewed venue. Reward depends on this reduction; its required efficiency cannot deal with the complexity of text in dialogue.

This authorship is a formality – a formal reference in a list of publications – but it is this that opens doors to careers and grants. It is the material focal point of the way scholarship is being managed. Writing and developing ideas – even sharing them in dialogue with others – is one thing. Having a formal and standardised reference to them is another. The difference between being an author of text and formal authorship is this: you have a hard time getting a job with a couple of manuscripts only, but you stand a chance applying with a proper personal list of publications that formally evidence the production of new information and *REFability*.

That which is accounted for formally can easily be categorised, sorted into abstract classes; it thereby appears to become meaningful in comparison. This is confronted with that which is elusive, non-formal, characterisable only by complexity and specificity. This is much less efficiently comparable. It remains – beyond the linearity of its material representation – dependent and contingent on the competence of the receiver. It does not have a surface that can be used for efficient measurement; it always remains ambiguous, chaotic, and idiosyncratic. The ephemeral character of thought and knowing can be fixed materially in text. But this substance requires qualitative engagement, dialogical opening towards meaning irrespective of materiality; oral, written, and residual text merge in this engagement. Publication establishing formal authorship, accumulated on personal CVs, or repackaged as potential for institutional (mock-)REF stars, can be measured efficiently. It transforms substance into formal significance. The development of formal rationality in modernity can be conceived of as a development of a dependency on such formal forms. It means making the incomparable comparable – of reducing everything to equivalence – and claiming its formal originality. The formal form allows for a reduction of abundancy by providing a means for efficient external calculability where there is mostly complexity and chaos internal to scholarship.

Formal authorship signposts that a scholar is knowledgeable, productive, and visible; that they can compete in the 'permanent competition *for* visibility' (Krüger and Hesselmann, 2020: 157; emphasis in original; translation by the author). Its focus shows a turning point from being visible in order to exhibit ideas, to deploying ideas in order to becoming visible. Above all, this visibility is signified by the venue. No one knows who has read text in evaluations, even for purposes of peer review; bibliometric accounts are, at the least, ambiguous in the humanities. Nevertheless, the high-ranking journal makes acceptable claims of visibility; it needs to do so since visibility depends on heuristics. And these heuristics make established venues the scaffolding of the establishment.

There are many new media in scholarly communication – new transformative technological environments – that potentially allow (aspiring) scholars to disseminate their ideas and arguments. These media have enabled new ways in which scholars *can* approach scholarship: it is easier to share initial ideas, to try provocative arguments, or to test the coherence of conceptions as they are shared informally via, for instance, blogs, social media, or preprint repositories. Scholars can make use of all sorts of digital tools that help them with what have formerly been core publishing activities such as writing, formatting, or disseminating work. These technologies have influenced practices in their own right; they enabled new practices. But they did not change the governance of scholarly work substantially; they did not open them up. Instead, the governance of individual scholarly work depends on the need to produce and put forward evidence of production in formal means of authorship more than ever. It is a sense of technological determinism to suggest that new technologies alone suffice to change this. Much rather, it is irrespective – or within some communities even because – of a new technology that the notion of output dominates. In other words: however worthwhile technology may be in a particular environment, conjuring up a utopia on technology compares to suggesting that the wind turbine alone will stop climate change. It will not do; governance and culture shape the use of technology and not vice versa.

This focus on technology can even go so far as to question the endeavour of the humanities generally. Adema exemplifies this in the technological utopia of a post-humanities, which is instructive for understanding the importance of our grasp of authorship. Common ownership, collaboration, and de-commodification are not mere means to achieve a liberation of the humanities from the powers of capitalist principles in a post-humanities critique. The means are used to liberate materiality itself. Technology shall enable new thinking through re-envisaged, digital spaces so that the material becomes alive. A performative author is constructed, a role that blurs the line of author and reader as all individuals are to engage openly in a mode of co-creation (Adema, 2021: 85–119). This seems worthwhile for the creation of art; its mode of sampling is widely employed. Moreover, it seems only justified to challenge the notion of the author as original inventor, as Adema does. Every author is embedded in intertextual references irrespective of this necessarily being materially inscribed; this is part of the ambivalence of authorship. But abolishing the author as a producer of text ushers in a highly individualistic agenda that inhibits intertextual reference and engagement in dialogue in the first place. Communities dissolve if authors who are responsible for their own utterances disappear within a cloud of unidentifiable voices. It fuels the individualism of production as it suggests that technology needs to be put in its place so that everyone can talk. But a fundamental problem of our scholarship is that content misses readers – those who engage with the complexity of the other *without* the constant desire to immediately imprint their own voices. The 'authorial output' that Adema (2021: 71) identifies as problematic is suggested to be problematic as it is an *authorial* voice. This dismisses that communities require authorial voices.

Authorship has gained its disproportionate momentum in the humanities as it is reduced to output, not as it is bounded by technology or by identifying as an *authorial* voice. Rather than trying to liberate technology, what is to be liberated is the interrelation of author and reader, the intertextuality that arises within the engagement of authors who contribute to an audience, and an audience that engages with an individual voice. Such a liberation would demand diminishing the overburdening of communication with other purposes. It would require avoiding recognising and rewarding formal output, and rather appreciating scholarship again – in the diversity of forms and contents in which it serves the advancement of knowing and understanding.

The formal author is like an aura that suppresses the speaking of the authorial voice and disguises appreciating the author in dialogue. With reference to Benjamin ([1935] 2010: 15), formal authorship evokes an appearance of equivalent nearness, however distant the content may be. This appearance diminishes the communicative complexity and qualitative contextuality of text. In the dialectical fashion of an aura, it carves out the content from its discursive context and intertextual references and, all the while, evokes its value from being placed within this tradition. This appearance suggests that the work can be reduced from complex ritual of scholarship to abstract comparison of its signification of new information.

The *job market* demands the operationalisation of this appearance. By so doing, it produces both the seductions and the pressures of a single market. It turns the recursion of dialogue into a self-referential dependency: output is produced so that output can be produced. The dialogical interrelation of the scholarship that precedes output – the dialogue that, at best, reaches society – stands in the shadow of this self-referential dependency. This creates the distance between the scholar subject and the intrinsic communicative purpose of text.

Self-Referentiality: The Distancing of Scholar and Text

The distancing of scholar and text is an alienated condition. The pressure determined in this book is an everyday idiom of alienation. Such pressure can be understood as an affect in practices that demands engagement that is perceived as not connecting to the substantive purposes of that practice. This often-slippery concept can be found throughout interpretations of modernity. May it be in grim practices of the individual who becomes 'dominated by the making of money' (Weber, [1905] 2001: 18), in the calculating, individuality erasing objectification of practices in the metropolis (Simmel, [1903] 2008), or, foremost, in the writings of Marx and Heidegger. Jaeggi overcomes these earlier conceptions by providing a social theoretical toolbox with which to comprehend what alienation may mean today. In short, it 'describes relations that are not entered into for their own sake, as well as activities with which one cannot "identify"' (Jaeggi, 2014: 4). This illuminates the disturbed relation of a subject to its practice: by doing something, the subject seems to be estranged from the purpose of so doing. Such relations are *mute* (Rosa, 2019: 305): they have lost purpose and the individual even becomes apathetic towards them irrespective of the result of action (such as economic benefit or social recognition). The frantic dash for ever more publications to compete on formal authorship shows the very characteristics described in these social theoretical accounts.

We can find the 'academic who publishes solely with a view towards the citation index' (Jaeggi, 2014: 4) as a phenomenon of alienation. Vostal (2016) also touches upon principles of alienation at several instances throughout his work on the experience of time and work in academia. Harvie (2000: 113) refers to researchers who are alienated from the products of their labour, the actual scholarship, since all that matters is produced output. And the sense of alienation is implied as the REF is said to lead to a 'compartmentalising of research into certain kinds of publication outputs, and an unhealthy climate of competition' (UCU, 2013: 45).

By instrumentalising publishing, negotiating quantity with quality, and steering scholarship so that it fits the demands of the job market instead of discourse, scholars reproduce the practices that lead to a *relation of relationlessness* (Jaeggi, 2014: 25). These practices are ingrained in a teleology of instrumental ends. The iron cage of formal rational terms seems difficult to escape. The road to engage in discourse is paved by rationalisation so that the will to publish as a non-strategic, communicative means cannot simply be actualised. Any aspiring scholar has to gain the advantage of a secure position for which they are required to publish in the first place. They need to utilise venues to make themselves visible and they need to prove themselves valuable for institutional positions by *having* output. Certainly, all of this does not work without an argument about history, a philosophical idea, a philological concept, or elsewise constituted substance; but such substance and the way they are borne by discourse do not suffice. The scholar has to feed formalised text into a great machine to prove that they *are there*, and to provide evidence that they *are competent in* the provision of something new.

Alienation matters as it indicates the futility of the practices – the futility of this feeding of a machine that is, most of all, self-referential. The principles embodied by publishing practices are shaped by an ideology of constant increase that is the operating mode of modernity. Underlying this is a notion of appropriation of the world by means of scientific-analytical progress (Rosa, 2019: 682). Such progress builds on the provision of instances of information. To explain a natural or social phenomenon in numbers and analytic abstraction results in a definite statement. It can be represented in text in the abstraction of methods and results. The more explanations being produced, the more statements may – though not necessarily do – follow. Weber explicated that this principle was inherent to research already a century ago (Weber, [1917] 2015: 16). The shift is that the humanities now have to conform to this principle, too, and the practices of publishing encompass this logic fundamentally.

The humanities do not operate such a mode of scientific progress, though. The ideas and arguments of earlier times are not historical relicts that are to be archived in the light of new information. Every new instance is not seen as being worth more than engagement with available content. Effectively shared research information does not sideline teaching. By the recursive structure of their discourses, the humanities exist through their histories. They advance by differentiation, by relating in dialogue to each other. Text, therefore, is relevant not as an instance of information that claims a truth here and now, until progress allows it to move on, but as having substantial meaning within a tradition of this differentiation.

Understanding is elusive as it is a competence, not an instance of information. Truth is not revealed as things to have; ideas are not mere takeaways. Text in the humanities does not state a result; it reflects the process of understanding. It is an approach to a representation of its revelation. Text is, in this sense, the death mask of the fluidity of a competence. To comprehend this revelation and experience, the competence behind it requires an audience to engage with its complexity and contextuality. Using thought as instance of information as a service is reductive translation. The humanities cannot be a service that can be employed as a direct means; it can always only be a dialogue from which something may be learned.

The engagement with complexity is circular: the author is no singular producer but themselves the entangled member of an audience. The constant focus on the production of something new disturbs this engagement. It claims that individuals simply *hold on* to knowledge instead of forming the intellectual capacity to understand and substantially teach others to do so. It demands innovation and shallow originality. This is the production of information in the sense of scientific progress, but not the representation of understanding in the intrinsic dialogical recursion of discourse communities. The 'cogency of a substantial piece of work seems more closely bound up with the individual voice of the author' (Collini, 2012: 75). The emphasis on measurable output opposes this and claims that text is an instance of objectifiable representation.

As both REF and *Exzellenzinitiative* show, such output production is made valuable for institutions and nations that operate in a realm of marketised education (Frank et al., 2019; Furedi, 2010). And, yet, they are not directly responsible for this marketisation. They merely exemplify a governance of scholarly work and academia generally. Particularly in the UK, this enforces the production of an excellence 'based on output measures' (Brink, 2018: 115). The strategic publishing encouraged by such performance measurement results in a form of *assembly line production* (Münch, 2011: 219). Output can be marketed as world-leading so that students and scholars apply for positions, or to be better positioned for various forms of material reward. But masses of scholars do not conduct better scholarship by producing masses of publications they have no time to engage with. Students do not learn more from masses of publications. They learn from better teaching and the deep engagement with complexity that a few texts suffice to provide; education builds upon dialogue (Freire, [1970] 2017). Society benefits from these students as they become teachers of the essential skills that are necessary to function in civil society, or from engagement with the enlightening, well-crafted texts in professional or crossover books.

The humanities are no project of a rush towards progress. They are, instead, the societal resource for maintaining senses for and of origins, as they teach historical-hermeneutical competence – the prowess to interpret and understand – which keeps origins alive and makes futures inhabitable; the 'humanities help the traditions, so that subjects can endure modernisations' (Marquard, 2020a: 178; translation by the author). This is reflected in the intertextuality of discourse, as Hyland suggests that 'new knowledge' in the humanities 'follows altogether more reiterative and recursive routes as writers retrace others' steps and revisit previously explored features' (Hyland, 1999: 353). Formal authorship is a neglect of this intertextuality. The latter requires engagement with difficulty and complexity. It is not efficient. But relentlessly increasing efficiency bears within it the mark of deficiency. Measuring intellectual achievement efficiently has come to favour marketable output so fundamentally that this favouring risks reducing individual authorship and publications to their antithetical irrelevance.

The fact that communication appears as commodifiable output is the result of a single, competitive market with marketable goods, price tags, and efficiently measurable value. These are principles shaping the practices and institutions in which society claims to understand what it means to be human. But this meaning cannot exist in instances of information. It requires an institutional setting that allows individuals to engage qualitatively and meaningfully to lay foundations for understanding. This is the ideal of the humanities' knowledge interest, its value for society: hermeneutic understanding 'makes possible the form of unconstrained consensus and the type of open intersubjectivity on which communicative action depends' (Habermas, 1971: 176). Issues of solidarity, social cohesion, and principles of equality cannot be answered with instances of information. They require dialogue.

This ideal needs to be reinstituted so that the governance and the recognition of scholarly work become reoriented towards complexity of understanding. It requires a shift towards more nuanced terms of competition and towards building an environment where scholars are allowed, even encouraged, to publish less. Such an institution may mean reducing input in order to regain an appreciation of complexity, the elusiveness of knowing, and the slow, intrinsically purposeful sharing of scholarship. It requires openness to the manifold ways in which communication may take place not just in technological means but in terms of recognition and reward. This might re-enable an appreciation of each publication as a substantial piece with a communicative purpose rooted in discourse, as well as allowing teaching and oral dialogue to take back their due space. It would be a strong step towards renewing the potential for purpose in the humanities, and for repairing the foundations of rational discourse within society.

Appendix

Detailed statistics to accompany the descriptive representations in the preceding chapters.

Table A1 Detailed statistics upon which Figures 2 and 3 are based.

		n	mean	sd	med	min	max	range	se
Germany	Humanities	17	2.94	1.71	2	1	7	6	0.42
		148	9.51	6.02	9	1	35	34	0.5
		34	13.3	5.94	12.5	7	32	25	1.02
		52	23.1	8.22	21.5	8	44	36	1.14
		106	26.1	8.57	24.5	10	50	40	0.83
	Soc sci	14	2.71	1.49	2	1	5	4	0.4
		86	7.45	4.73	7	0	25	25	0.51
		26	10.8	4.39	10	4	20	16	0.86
		18	18.6	8.28	17	6	38	32	1.95
		44	23.1	9.99	21	10	60	50	1.51
UK	Humanities	13	4.62	5.5	3	1	22	21	1.53
		94	10.5	5.71	9.5	1	32	31	0.59
		80	19	8.2	18	5	40	35	0.92
		61	33	7.15	32	20	50	30	0.92
	Soc sci	13	7.92	8.15	5	1	30	29	2.26
		89	9.09	3.99	9	2	20	18	0.42
		66	17.4	8.04	16.5	3	42	39	0.99
		56	27.4	9.98	25.5	7	52	45	1.33

Table A2 Detailed statistics upon which Figure 33 is based.

	n	mean	sd	med	min	max	range	se
Germany, no pressure	107	23.59	10.43	24	2	50	48	1.01
UK, no pressure	50	26.62	12.03	27	4	50	46	1.7
Germany, low pressure	159	15.96	9.55	14	2	45	43	0.76
UK, low pressure	114	19.58	11.12	17.5	1	45	44	1.04
Germany, high pressure	74	10.32	6.44	10	1	35	34	0.75
UK, high pressure	71	13.54	7.62	12	1	40	39	0.9

Table A3 Structured questionnaire of the quantitative survey

	Item	Question	Type
General	Gender	What's your gender?	closed (female, male, other)
	Age	How old are you?	open
	Active	For how many years have you been active as a researcher?	open
	Career position	Please indicate which of the following best describes your current academic level (multiple answers possible)	closed (from junior to senior/tenured, incl. open other option)
	Discipline	Please indicate which discipline you are mainly working in (for instance, philosophy, linguistics, mathematics, history, nuclear physics, information studies, etc.)	open
	Cluster	Do you consider yourself a researcher in the...	closed (Humanities, Social Sciences, Arts, etc., incl. open other option)
	Affiliation	What kind of institution are you affiliated with?	closed (country-specific types of institutions such as Russell Group, New University in the UK or Excellence University in Germany)
Portfolio	Articles	How many articles in scholarly journals have you published in your career so far?	closed (0, 1-9, 10-19, 20-29, 30-49, >50)
	Contributions	How many contributions to edited volumes have you published in your career so far?	closed (0, 1-9, 10-19, 20-29, 30-49, >50)
	Monographs	How many edited volumes did you edit/oversee in your career so far?	closed (0, 1-9, 10-19, 20-29, 30-49, >50)
	Textbooks	How many monographs have you published in your career so far?	closed (0, 1-2, 3-5, 6-9, 10-15, 16-24, >25)
	Editor	How many textbooks have you published in your career so far?	closed (0, 1-2, 3-5, 6-9, 10-15, 16-24, >25)
	Articles OA	Have you published any of your articles Open Access so far?	closed (Yes, No, Not applicable)
	Monographs OA	Have you published any of your monographs Open Access so far?	closed (Yes, No, Not applicable)
	Popular books	Have you published any non-scholarly books that deal with your research?	closed (Yes, No)
	Blog	Do you publish in an online blog on a regular basis?	closed (No, Yes, my own blog, Yes, a collaborative blog)
	Other non-traditional	Have you published in any other non-traditional format, where the content deals with your research? If so, please indicate:	open
	Language	Do you usually publish in English or German language?	closed (English, German, Both, depending on the research, incl. open other option)
	Second Language	Is this a second language for you?	closed (Yes, No)
Publishing Pressure	Affected by REF	My publication behaviour is affected by official research assessments (for instance, the REF in the UK, or the *Exzellenzinitiative* in Germany)	closed (Yes, negatively; Yes, positively; No; I don't know)
	Publish article	I feel pressured to publish more journal articles	Likert scale
	Publish monograph	I feel pressured to publish a monograph	Likert scale
	Publish OA	I feel pressured to publish Open Access	Likert scale
	Publish faster	I feel pressured to publish faster so that the quality of the research suffers	Likert scale

Publishing Perception	Publish faster REF	I feel pressured to publish faster so that the publications can be included in research assessments (for instance, the REF in the UK or the *Exzellenzinitiative* in Germany)	Likert scale
	Publish fewer	If I had the choice, I'd publish fewer articles or contributions to focus on a monograph	Likert scale
	Single authorship	Single authorship is predominant in my area of research	Likert scale
	New articles	Too many new articles are being published each year in my area of research	Likert scale
	New monographs	Too many new monographs are being published each year in my area of research	Likert scale
	Metrics for books	I know/follow the development of metrics (for instance, citations or downloads) of my books	Likert scale
	Metrics for articles	I know/follow the development of metrics (for instance, the Impact Factor, citations, downloads) of my articles (journals respectively)	Likert scale
	Quantifiable value	The value of research in my area of research can well be expressed in quantifiers/metrics	Likert scale
	Salami slicing	Salami slicing (making as many publications as possible out of a single analysis or finding) is common in my area of research	Likert scale
	Monograph	Research in my area of research can best be expressed with a monograph	Likert scale
	Publication list	My career is built on my strong publication list	Likert scale
	Publisher brand	A publisher's brand is an important indicator for quality when I'm browsing through a bibliography	Likert scale
For my next monograph...	Selfpublishing	I would publish my next monograph with a self-publishing service (i.e. without a traditional publisher).	closed (Yes, No, I don't know)
	Rapid publication	Rapid publication process focussing on immediacy	Scale (importance)
	Bookshop	Availability in bookshops	Scale (importance)
	OA publication	Unhurried publication process focussing on content improvement	Scale (importance)
	Unhurried publication	Discoverability in online databases	Scale (importance)
	Availability in library	Open Access publication	Scale (importance)
	Discoverability online	Availability in physical form in libraries	Scale (importance)
	Comment	Any other comments?	open

References

Acton SE, Bell AJ, Toseland CP, et al. (2019) A survey of new PIs in the UK. *eLife* 8: e46827. https://doi.org/10.7554/eLife.46827.

Adema J (2021) *Living books: Experiments in the posthumanities*. Cambridge, MA: MIT Press.

Adema J and Moore SA (2018) Collectivity and collaboration: Imagining new forms of communality to create resilience in scholar-led publishing. *Insights: The UKSG Journal* 31(3): 1–11. https://doi.org/10.1629/uksg.399.

Agarwal A (2015) Wissenschaftler: Die Rebellion der Doktoranden. *Die Zeit*. www.zeit.de/2015/06/wissenschaftler-petition-arbeitsbedingungen (accessed 24 June 2020).

Aitkenhead D (2013) Peter Higgs: I wouldn't be productive enough for today's academic system. *The Guardian*. www.theguardian.com/science/2013/dec/06/peter-higgs-boson-academic-system (accessed 3 December 2019).

Akbaritabar A and Squazzoni F (2020) Gender patterns of publication in top sociological journals. *Science, Technology, & Human Values* 46(3): 555–76. https://doi.org/10.1177/0162243920941588.

Ambrasat J and Heger C (2020) Barometer für die Wissenschaft: Ergebnisse der Wissenschaftsbefragung 2019/20. *Deutsches Zentrum für Hochschul- und Wissenschaftsforschung GmbH*. www.wb.dzhw.eu/downloads/wibef_barometer2020.pdf (accessed 17 December 2020).

Anonymous academic (2018) They called my university a PhD factory – now I understand why. *The Guardian*. www.theguardian.com/higher-education-network/2018/mar/23/they-called-my-university-a-phd-factory-now-i-understand-why (accessed 24 June 2020).

Anonymous editorial (2019) The mental health of PhD researchers demands urgent attention. *Nature* 575(7782): 257–8. https://doi.org/10.1038/d41586-019-03489-1.

Archer L (2008) Younger academics' constructions of 'authenticity', 'success' and professional identity. *Studies in Higher Education* 33(4): 385–403. https://doi.org/10.1080/03075070802211729.

Arnold E, Simmonds P, Farla K, et al. (2018) Review of the Research Excellence Framework: Evidence report. *technopolis group*. https://assets.publishing.service.gov.uk/government/uploads/system/uploads/attachment_data/file/768162/research-excellence-framework-review-evidence-report.pdf (accessed 30 October 2019).

Aufderheide E and Neizert B (2016) Internationalisierung der Forschung. In Simon D, Knie A, Hornbostel S and Zimmermann K (eds) *Handbuch Wissenschaftspolitik*. Wiesbaden: Verlag für Sozialwissenschaften, pp. 335–54.

Bacevic J (2019) War on universities? Neoliberalism, intellectual positioning, and knowledge production in the UK. Doctoral thesis, University of Cambridge. www.repository.cam.ac.uk/handle/1810/295777 (accessed 29 March 2023).

Bacevic J and Muellerleile C (2017) The moral economy of open access. *European Journal of Social Theory* 21(2): 169–88. https://doi.org/10.1177/1368431017717368.

Bahr A, Eichhoren K, and Kubon S (2021) #IchBinHanna. https://ichbinhanna.wordpress.com/ (accessed 22 October 2021).

Baker S (2020a) Sudden shift to teaching-only contracts ahead of REF census. *Times Higher Education*. www.timeshighereducation.com/news/sudden-shift-teaching-only-contracts-ahead-ref-census (accessed 17 September 2020).

(2020b) Teaching-only contracts up again as REF approaches. *Times Higher Education*. www.timeshighereducation.com/news/teaching-only-contracts-again-ref-approaches (accessed 17 September 2020).

Barnes L and Gatti R (2019) Bibliodiversity in practice: Developing community-owned, open infrastructures to unleash open access publishing. ELPUB 2019 23rd International Conference on Electronic Publishing, June 2019, Marseille, France. https://hcommons.org/?get_group_doc=1003561/1593595567-oep-9940.pdf (accessed 29 March 2023).

Barth A (2019) *Publish or perish! Ein Schwarzbuch der Wissenschaft.* Nordhausen: Verlag Traugott Bautz.

Baveye PC (2014) Learned publishing: Who still has time to read? *Learned Publishing* 27(1): 48–51. https://doi.org/10.1087/20140107.

Beard M (2019) No competitive martyrdom. *Times Literary Supplement.* www.the-tls.co.uk/articles/no-competitive-martyrdom/ (accessed 20 December 2019).

Belfiore E (2013) The 'rhetoric of gloom' v. the discourse of impact in the humanities: Stuck in a deadlock? In Belfiore E and Upchurch A (eds) *Humanities in the twenty-first century: Beyond utility and markets.* Manchester: Manchester University Press, pp. 17–43.

Bence V and Oppenheim C (2005) The evolution of the UK's Research Assessment Exercise: Publications, performance and perceptions. *Journal of Educational Administration and History* 37(2): 137–55. https://doi.org/10.1080/00220620500211189.

Bendels MHK, Müller R, Brueggmann D, et al. (2018) Gender disparities in high-quality research revealed by Nature Index journals. *PLOS ONE* 13(1): e0189136. https://doi.org/10.1371/journal.pone.0189136.

Benjamin W ([1935] 2010) The work of art in the age of its technological reproducibility [first version]. *Grey Room* 39(Spring): 11–38. https://doi.org/10.1162/grey.2010.1.39.11.

Biagioli M (2016) Watch out for cheats in citation game. *Nature* 535(7611): 201. https://doi.org/10.1038/535201a.

Biggs M (2009) Self-fulfilling prophecies. In Hedström P and Bearman P (eds) *The Oxford handbook of analytical sociology*. Oxford: Oxford University Press, pp. 294–314.

Boehm G (2009) Kunstwissenschaft. In Schütte G and Schuh C (eds) *Publikationsverhalten in unterschiedlichen wissenschaftlichen Disziplinen: Beiträge zur Beurteilung von Forschungsleistungen*. Diskussionspapiere der Alexander von Humboldt-Stiftung [Discussion Papers of the Alexander von Humboldt Foundation], Bonn, pp. 62–3.

Borenstein J and Shamoo AE (2015) Rethinking authorship in the era of collaborative research. *Accountability in Research* 22(5): 267–83. https://doi.org/10.1080/08989621.2014.968277.

Bornmann L, Mutz R, and Daniel H-D (2007) Gender differences in grant peer review: A meta-analysis. *Journal of Informetrics* 1(3): 226–38. https://doi.org/10.1016/j.joi.2007.03.001.

Bourdieu P (1980) The production of belief: Contribution to an economy of symbolic goods. *Media, Culture & Society* 2(3): 261–93. https://doi.org/10.1177/016344378000200305.

(1988) *Homo academicus*. Stanford, CA: Stanford University Press.

(1998) *Practical reason: On the theory of action*. Stanford, CA: Stanford University Press.

(2006) *The rules of art: Genesis and structure of the literary field*. Stanford, CA: Stanford University Press.

(2013) Symbolic capital and social classes. *Journal of Classical Sociology* 13(2): 292–302. https://doi.org/10.1177/1468795X12468736.

Brechelmacher A, Park E, Ates G, et al. (2015) The rocky road to tenure: Career paths in academia. In Fumasoli T, Goastellec G, and Kehm B (eds) *Academic work and careers in Europe: Trends, challenges, perspectives*. Heidelberg: Springer, pp. 13–40.

Brink C (2018) *The soul of a university: Why excellence is not enough*. Bristol: Bristol University Press.

British Academy (2019) A commentary by the British Academy on cOAlition S's final version of Plan S. www.thebritishacademy.ac.uk/documents/283/A_commentary_by_the_British_Academy_on_final_Plan_S-July_2019.pdf (accessed 22 June 2020).

Bruni R, Catalano G, Daraio C, et al. (2020) Studying the heterogeneity of European higher education institutions. *Scientometrics* 125(2): 1117–44. https://doi.org/10.1007/s11192-020-03717-w.

Budapest (2002) Budapest open access initiative. www.budapestopenaccessinitiative.org/read (accessed 25 January 2020).

Calkin S (2013) The academic career path has been thoroughly destabilised by the precarious practices of the neoliberal university. *LSE Impact of Social Sciences Blog*. https://blogs.lse.ac.uk/impactofsocialsciences/2013/11/01/precarity-and-the-neoliberal-university/ (accessed 24 June 2020).

Collini S (2012) *What are universities for?* London: Penguin Books.

Colpaert J (2012) The 'publish and perish' syndrome. *Computer Assisted Language Learning* 25(5): 383–91. https://doi.org/10.1080/09588221.2012.735101.

Colquhoun D (2011) Publish-or-perish: Peer review and the corruption of science. *The Guardian*. www.theguardian.com/science/2011/sep/05/publish-perish-peer-review-science (accessed 3 December 2019).

Crane T (2018) The philosopher's tone. *Times Literary Supplement*. www.the-tls.co.uk/articles/public/philosophy-journals-review/ (accessed 17 September 2019).

Crossick G (2016) Monographs and open access. *Insights: The UKSG Journal* 29(1): 14–19. https://doi.org/10.1629/uksg.280.

Dean D (2018) The 2021 REF will concentrate funding even further. *Times Higher Education*. www.timeshighereducation.com/opinion/2021-

ref-will-concentrate-funding-even-further (accessed 17 September 2020).

DFG (2018) *Entscheidungen in der Exzellenzstrategie: Exzellenzkommission wählt 57 Exzellenzcluster aus.* www.dfg.de/service/presse/pressemitteilungen/2018/pressemitteilung_nr_43/index.html (accessed 23 October 2021).

Dilthey W ([1910] 1970) *Der Aufbau der geschichtlichen Welt in den Geisteswissenschaften.* Frankfurt: Suhrkamp.

Dix A (2016) Evaluating research assessment: Metrics-based analysis exposes implicit bias in REF2014 results. *LSE Impact of Social Sciences Blog.* https://blogs.lse.ac.uk/impactofsocialsciences/2016/03/22/ref2014-and-computer-science-and-informatics-subpanel/ (accessed 11 September 2020).

DORA (2012) San Francisco Declaration on Research Assessment. https://sfdora.org/read/ (accessed 10 August 2020).

Drees WB (2021) *What are the humanities for?* Cambridge: Cambridge University Press.

Evans TM, Bira L, Gastelum JB, et al. (2018) Evidence for a mental health crisis in graduate education. *Nature Biotechnology* 36(3): 282–4. https://doi.org/10.1038/nbt.4089.

Eve MP (2019a) Comments on the interim Royal Historical Society response to Plan S. https://eve.gd/2019/01/17/comments-on-the-interim-royal-historical-society-response-to-plan-s/ (accessed 22 June 2020).

(2019b) The British Academy response misrepresents Plan S and OA. https://eve.gd/2019/07/24/the-british-academy-response-misrepresents-plan-s-and-oa/ (accessed 22 June 2020).

Falk-Krzesinski HJ, Contractor N, Fiore SM, et al. (2011) Mapping a research agenda for the science of team science. *Research Evaluation* 20(2): 145–58. https://doi.org/10.3152/095820211X12941371876580.

Finch J (2012) Accessibility, sustainability, excellence: How to expand access to research publications. Report of the Working Group on Expanding

Access to Published Research Findings. www.acu.ac.uk/research-information-network/finch-report-final (accessed 12 December 2018).

Fish S (2008) Will the humanities save us? *The New York Times*. https://opinionator.blogs.nytimes.com/2008/01/06/will-the-humanities-save-us/ (accessed 7 December 2017).

Flaherty C (2020) Early journal submission data suggest COVID-19 is tanking women's research productivity. *Inside Higher Ed*. www.insidehighered.com/news/2020/04/21/early-journal-submission-data-suggest-covid-19-tanking-womens-research-productivity (accessed 24 June 2020).

Fohrmann J (2009) Literaturwissenschaft. In Schütte G and Schuh C (eds) *Publikationsverhalten in unterschiedlichen wissenschaftlichen Disziplinen: Beiträge zur Beurteilung von Forschungsleistungen*. Diskussionspapiere der Alexander von Humboldt-Stiftung [Discussion Papers of the Alexander von Humboldt Foundation], Bonn, pp. 50–3.

Foucault M (1979) What is an author? *Screen* 20(1). https://doi.org/10.1093/screen/20.1.13.

Franck G (1999) Scientific communication: A vanity fair? *Science* 286(5437): 53–5. https://doi.org/10.1126/science.286.5437.53.

Franco-Santos M and Doherty N (2017) Performance management and well-being: A close look at the changing nature of the UK higher education workplace. *International Journal of Human Resource Management* 28(16): 2319–50. https://doi.org/10.1080/09585192.2017.1334148.

Frank J, Gowar N, and Naef M (2019) *English universities in crisis: Markets without competition*. Bristol: Bristol University Press.

Freire P ([1970] 2017) *Pedagogy of the oppressed*. London: Penguin Books.

Furedi F (2010) Introduction to the marketisation of higher education and the student as consumer. In Molesworth M, Nixon E, and Scullion R (eds) *The marketisation of higher education and the student as consumer*. London: Routledge, pp. 1–8.

Garland R (2012) The humanities: Plain and simple. *Arts and Humanities in Higher Education* 11(3): 300–12. https://doi.org/10.1177/147402221 2438754.

Glatthorn AA (2002) *Publish or perish: The educator's imperative.* Thousand Oaks, CA: Corwin Press.

Grove J (2020) Leading UK universities spend £49 million on pre-REF job cuts. *Times Higher Education.* www.timeshighereducation.com/news/leading-uk-universities-spend-ps49-million-pre-ref-job-cuts (accessed 17 September 2020).

Guraya SY, Norman RI, Khoshhal KI, et al. (2016) Publish or perish mantra in the medical field: A systematic review of the reasons, consequences and remedies. *Pakistan Journal of Medical Sciences* 32 (6): 1562–7. https://doi.org/10.12669/pjms.326.10490.

Habermas J (1971) *Knowledge and human interests.* Boston, MA: Beacon Press.

Hamann J (2009) *Der Preis des Erfolges: Die 'Krise der Geisteswissenschaften' in feldtheoretischer Perspektive.* Bamberg: University of Bamberg Press.

Hamann J and Zimmer LM (2017) The internationality imperative in academia: The ascent of internationality as an academic virtue. *Higher Education Research & Development* 36(7): 1418–32. https://doi.org/10.1080/07294360.2017.1325849.

Harvie D (2000) Alienation, class and enclosure in UK universities. *Capital & Class* 24(2): 103–32. https://doi.org/10.1177/030981680007100105.

Harzing A-W (2016) *The publish or perish tutorial: 80 easy tips to get the best out of the publish or perish software.* London: Tarma Software Research.

Henkel M (1999) The modernisation of research evaluation: The case of the UK. *Higher Education* 38(1): 105–22. https://doi.org/10.1023/A:1003799013939.

Hexter JH (1969) Publish or perish – A defense. *The Public Interest* 17: 60–78. https://search.proquest.com/docview/1298134010?accoun tid=14511 (accessed 29 March 2023).

Hicks D (2012) Performance-based university research funding systems. *Research Policy* 41(2): 251–61. https://doi.org/10.1016/j.respol.2011 .09.007.

Hills P (ed) (1987) *Publish or perish*. Soham, UK: Peter Francis Publishers.

Honneth A (2003) Redistribution as recognition. In Fraser N and Honneth A (eds) *Redistribution or recognition? A political-philosophical exchange*. London: Verso, pp. 110–97.

Humboldt W von ([1810] 2017) Über die innere und äußere Organisation der höheren wissenschaftlichen Anstalten in Berlin. In Lauer G (ed) *Schriften zur Bildung*. Stuttgart: Reclam, pp. 152–65.

Hundley V, Teijlingen E, and Simkhada P (2013) Academic authorship: Who, why and in what order? *Health Renaissance* 11(2). https://doi .org/10.3126/hren.v11i2.8214.

Hyland K (1999) Academic attribution: Citation and the construction of disciplinary knowledge. *Applied Linguistics* 20(3): 341–67. https:// doi.org/10.1093/applin/20.3.341.

(2015) *Academic publishing: Issues and challenges in the construction of knowledge*. Oxford: Oxford University Press.

Jaeggi R (2014) *Alienation*. New York: Columbia University Press.

Jehne M (2009) Geschichtswissenschaft. In Schütte G and Schuh C (eds) *Publikationsverhalten in unterschiedlichen wissenschaftlichen Disziplinen: Beiträge zur Beurteilung von Forschungsleistungen*. Diskussionspapiere der Alexander von Humboldt-Stiftung [Discussion Papers of the Alexander von Humboldt Foundation], Bonn, pp. 59–61.

Jubb M (2017) Academic books and their futures: A report to the AHRC and the British Library. *Academic Book of the Future*. https://acade

micbookfuture.files.wordpress.com/2017/06/academic-books-and-their-futures_jubb1.pdf (accessed 31 October 2018).

Jump P (2013) Evolution of the REF. *Times Higher Education*. www.time shighereducation.com/features/evolution-of-the-ref/2008100.article (accessed 21 June 2021).

Kagan J (2009) *The three cultures: Natural sciences, social sciences, and the humanities in the 21st century*. Cambridge: Cambridge University Press.

Karabel J (2005) *The chosen: The hidden history of admission and exclusion at Harvard, Yale, and Princeton*. Boston, MA: Houghton Mifflin.

Kelsky K (2015) *The professor is in: The essential guide to turning your Ph.D. into a job*. New York: Three Rivers Press.

Knoche M (2019) Kritik der politischen Ökonomie der Wissenschaftskommunikation als Ideologiekritik: Open Access. In Krüger U and Sevignani S (eds) *Ideologie, Kritik, Öffentlichkeit: Verhandlungen des Netzwerks Kritische Kommunikationswissenschaft*. Leipzig University, pp. 140–74. https://doi.org/10.36730/ideologiekritik.2019.0

Knöchelmann M (2019) Open science in the humanities, or: Open humanities? *Publications* 7(4). https://doi.org/10.3390/publications 7040065.

   (2021a) Systemimmanenz und Transformation: Die Bibliothek der Zukunft als lokale Verwalterin? Preprint version. *Bibliothek Forschung und Praxis* 45(1). https://doi.org/10.1515/bfp-2020-0101.

   (2021b) The democratisation myth: Open access and the solidification of epistemic injustices. *Science & Technology Studies* 34(2): 65–89. https://doi.org/10.23987/sts.94964.

Knöchelmann M and Schendzielorz C (2023) Writing in the sciences: Scientists as writers, scientific writing, and the persuasive story. *SocArXiv*. https://doi.org/10.31235/osf.io/fmcsp.

Könneker C (2018) Das 'Publish or perish' Diktat muss enden. *Spektrum der Wissenschaft.* www.spektrum.de/kolumne/das-publish-or-perish-diktat-muss-enden/1579710 (accessed 3 December 2019).

Kristof N (2014) Professors, we need you! *The New York Times.* www.nytimes.com/2014/02/16/opinion/sunday/kristof-professors-we-need-you.html (accessed 3 December 2019).

Kruger P (2018) Why it is not a 'failure' to leave academia. *Nature* 560 (7716): 133–4. https://doi.org/10.1038/d41586-018-05838-y.

Krüger AK and Hesselmann F (2020) Sichtbarkeit und Bewertung. *Zeitschrift für Soziologie* 49(2–3): 145–63. https://doi.org/10.1515/zfsoz-2020-0015.

Larivière V, Ni C, Gingras Y, et al. (2013) Bibliometrics: Global gender disparities in science. *Nature* 504(7479): 211–13. https://doi.org/10.1038/504211a.

Laufenberg M, Erlemann M, Norkus M, et al. (2018) *Prekäre Gleichstellung: Geschlechtergerechtigkeit, soziale Ungleichheit und unsichere Arbeitsverhältnisse in der Wissenschaft.* Wiesbaden: Verlag für Sozialwissenschaften.

Lee I (2014) Publish or perish: The myth and reality of academic publishing. *Language Teaching* 47(2): 250–61. https://doi.org/10.1017/S0261444811000504.

Levecque K, Anseel F, Beuckelaer A de, et al. (2017) Work organization and mental health problems in PhD students. *Research Policy* 46(4): 868–79. https://doi.org/10.1016/j.respol.2017.02.008.

Liessmann KP (2006) *Theorie der Unbildung: Die Irrtümer der Wissensgesellschaft.* Vienna: Zsolnay.

Lipsett A (2007) RAE selection gets brutal. *Times Higher Education.* www.timeshighereducation.com/news/rae-selection-gets-brutal/207648.article (accessed 25 October 2019).

Lorenz C (2012) If you're so smart, why are you under surveillance? Universities, neoliberalism, and new public management. *Critical Inquiry* 38(3): 599–629. https://doi.org/10.1086/664553.

Lussier RN (2010) *Publish don't perish: 100 tips that improve your ability to get published*. Charlotte, NC: Information Age Publishing.

Maher B and Sureda Anfres M (2016) Young scientists under pressure: What the data show. *Nature* 538(7626): 444. https://doi.org/10.1038/538444a.

Mandler P (2020) *Crisis of the meritocracy: Britain's transition to mass education since the Second World War*. Oxford: Oxford University Press.

Markovits D (2020) *The meritocracy trap*. London: Penguin Books.

Marquard O (2020a) Über die Unvermeidlichkeit der Geisteswissenschaften. In Marquard O (ed) *Zukunft braucht Herkunft: Philosophische Essays*. Ditzingen: Reclam, pp. 171–89.

(2020b) Zukunft braucht Herkunft: Philosophische Betrachtungen über Modernität und Menschlichkeit. In Marquard O (ed) *Zukunft braucht Herkunft: Philosophische Essays*. Ditzingen: Reclam, pp. 236–48.

Martin BR (2011) The Research Excellence Framework and the 'impact agenda': Are we creating a Frankenstein monster? *Research Evaluation* 20(3): 247–54. https://doi.org/10.3152/095820211X13118583635693.

Marx K ([1867] 1906) *Capital: A critique of political economy*. New York: Random House.

McNulty Y (2013) Publish don't perish: 100 tips that improve your ability to get published by Robert N. Lussier, Information Age Publishing Inc., 2010 (new edition), 195 pp, soft cover, ISBN: 978-1-61735-113-6. *Journal of Management & Organization* 19(2): 238–40. https://doi.org/10.1017/jmo.2013.22.

Merton RK (1948) The self-fulfilling prophecy. *The Anioch Review* 8(2): 193–210.

(1968) The Matthew effect in science: The reward and communication systems of science are considered. *Science* 159(3810): 56–63. https://doi.org/10.1126/science.159.3810.56.

Meyer JW and Rowan B (1977) Institutionalized oganizations: Formal structure as myth and ceremony. *American Journal of Sociology* 83(2): 340–63. https://doi.org/10.1086/226550.

Miller AN, Taylor SG and Bedeian AG (2011) Publish or perish: Academic life as management faculty live it. *Career Development International* 16(5): 422–45. https://doi.org/10.1108/13620431111167751.

Moore S (2019) Common struggles: Policy-based vs. scholar-led approaches to open access in the humanities. *Humanities Commons.* http://dx.doi.org/10.17613/st5m-cx33 (accessed 1 April 2020).

Moore S, Neylon C, Eve MP, et al. (2016) 'Excellence R Us': University research and the fetishisation of excellence. *Palgrave Communications* 3. https://doi.org/10.1057/palcomms.2016.105.

Moosa IA (2018) *Publish or perish: Perceived benefits versus unintended consequences.* Cheltenham, UK: Edward Elgar Publishing.

Moss-Racusin CA, Dovidio JF, Brescoll VL, et al. (2012) Science faculty's subtle gender biases favor male students. *Proceedings of the National Academy of Sciences* 109(41): 16474–9. https://doi.org/10.1073/pnas.1211286109.

Münch R (2007) *Die akademische Elite: Zur sozialen Konstruktion wissenschaftlicher Exzellenz.* Frankfurt: Suhrkamp.

(2008) *Globale Eliten, lokale Autoritäten: Politik unter dem Regime von Pisa, McKinsey & Co.* Frankfurt: Suhrkamp.

(2011) *Akademischer Kapitalismus: Zur politischen Ökonomie der Hochschulreform.* Berlin: Suhrkamp.

Natale E (2019) In open access's long shadow: A view from the humanities. *Zeitschrift für Bibliothekskultur* 6(1): 24–47. https://doi.org/10.12685/027.7-6-1-184.

Pasternack P (2008) Die Exzellenzinitiative als politisches Programm. In Bloch R, Keller A, Lottmann A and Würmann C (eds) *Making excellence: Grundlagen, praxis und Konsequenzen*. Bielefeld: wbv Media, pp. 13–36. https://doi.org/10.3278/6001589w013.

Pauli R (2016) Professorin über akademisches Prekariat: 'Bestenfalls eine Kopierkarte'. *taz*. https://taz.de/Professorin-ueber-akademisches-Prekariat/!5321695/ (accessed 24 June 2020).

Pörksen B (2015) Wissenschaft: Wo seid ihr, Professoren? *Die Zeit*. www.zeit.de/2015/31/wissenschaft-professoren-engagement-oekonomie/komplettansicht (accessed 3 December 2019).

Ramdarshan Bold M (2018) The return of the social author. *Convergence: The International Journal of Research into New Media Technologies* 24 (2): 117–36. https://doi.org/10.1177/1354856516654459.

Readings B (1999) *The university in ruins*. Cambridge, MA: Harvard University Press.

Reckwitz A (2020) *Das hybride Subjekt: Eine Theorie der Subjektkulturen von der bürgerlichen Moderne zur Postmoderne*. Berlin: Suhrkamp.

REF (2014) Research Excellence Framework 2014: The results. www.ref.ac.uk/2014/media/ref/content/pub/REF%2001%202014%20-%20full%20document.pdf (accessed 9 October 2020).

(2020a) About. www.ref.ac.uk/about/ (accessed 17 July 2020).

(2020b) What is the REF? www.ref.ac.uk/about/what-is-the-ref/ (accessed 17 July 2020).

(2020c) REF 2021: Draft guidance on submissions. www.ref.ac.uk/media/1092/ref-2019_01-guidance-on-submissions.pdf (accessed 12 November 2020).

Relman A (1977) Publish or perish – or both. *New England Journal of Medicine* 297: 724–5. www.nejm.org/doi/full/10.1056/NEJM197709292971313.

Rescher N (2019) Die Fragmentierung der gegenwärtigen Philosophie am Beispiel der Philosophiegeschichte. *Deutsche Zeitschrift für Philosophie* 66(6): 747–63. https://doi.org/10.1515/dzph-2018-0054.

Rond M de and Miller AN (2005) Publish or perish. *Journal of Management Inquiry* 14(4): 321–9. https://doi.org/10.1177/1056492605276850.

Rosa H (2010) *Alienation and acceleration: Towards a critical theory of late-modern temporality*. Malmö: NSU Press.

—— (2019) *Resonanz: Eine Soziologie der Weltbeziehung*. Berlin: Suhrkamp.

Royal Historical Society (2019) Plan S and history journals. https://royalhistsoc.org/policy/publication-open-access/plan-s-and-history-journals/ (accessed 22 June 2020).

Rusconi A, Netz N, and Solga H (2020) Publizieren im Lockdown Erfahrungen von Professorinnen und Professoren. *WZB Mitteilungen* 170: 24–6. https://bibliothek.wzb.eu/artikel/2020/f-23507.pdf (accessed 29 March 2023).

Sandel MJ (2020) *The tyranny of merit: What's become of the common good?* London: Allen Lane.

Sander N (2017) *Das akademische Prekariat: Leben zwischen Frist und Plan*. Cologne: Herbert von Halem Verlag.

Schneijderberg C, Götze N and Müller L (2022) A study of 25 years of publication outputs in the German academic profession. *Scientometrics*. https://doi.org/10.1007/s11192-021-04216-2.

Schroder S, Welter F, Leisten I, et al. (2014) Research performance and evaluation: Empirical results from collaborative research centers and clusters of excellence in Germany. *Research Evaluation* 23(3): 221–32. https://doi.org/10.1093/reseval/rvu010.

Segran E (2014) What can you do with a humanities Ph.D., anyway? *The Atlantic*. www.theatlantic.com/business/archive/2014/03/what-can-you-do-with-a-humanities-phd-anyway/359927/ (accessed 24 June 2020).

Shackleton JR and Booth P (2015) Abolishing the higher education Research Excellence Framework. *Institute of Economic Affairs*. www.iea.org.uk/sites/default/files/publications/files/REF%20BRIEFING%20FINAL.pdf (accessed 9 November 2020).

Siegel V (2008) Where credit is due. *Disease Models & Mechanisms* 1(4–5): 187–91. https://doi.org/10.1242/dmm.002055.

Simmel G ([1903] 2008) Die Großstädte und das Geistesleben. In Simmel G (ed) *Individualismus der modernen Zeit: Und andere soziologische Abhandlungen*. Frankfurt: Suhrkamp, pp. 319–33.

Small H (2013) *The value of the humanities*. Oxford: Oxford University Press.

Sondermann M, Simon D, Scholz A-M, et al. (2008) Die Exzellenzinitiative: Beobachtungen aus der Implementierungsphase. iFQ-Working Paper. www.forschungsinfo.de/Publikationen/Download/working_paper_5_2008.pdf.

Specht J, Hof C, Tjus J, et al. (2017) Departments statt Lehrstühle: Moderne Personalstruktur für eine zukunftsfähige Wissenschaft. *Die Junge Akademie*. www.diejungeakademie.de/fileadmin/user_upload/Dokumente/aktivitaeten/wissenschaftspolitik/stellungnahmen_broscheuren/JA_Debattenbeitrag_Department-Struktur.pdf (accessed 23 October 2021).

Stekeler-Weithofer P (2009) Das Problem der Evaluation von Beiträgen zur Philosophie Ein streitbarer Zwischenruf. *Deutsche Zeitschrift für Philosophie* 57(1). https://doi.org/10.1524/dzph.2009.57.1.149.

Swain H (2013) Zero hours in universities: 'You never know if it'll be enough to survive'. *The Guardian*. www.theguardian.com/education/2013/sep/16/zero-hours-contracts-at-universities (accessed 24 June 2020).

Thomä D (2019) Geist, Kultur, Gesellschaft. Zur Begründung und Kritik von Geisteswissenschaft. In Joas H and Noller J (eds) *Geisteswissenschaft-*

was bleibt? Zwischen Theorie, Tradition und Transformation. Freiburg: Verlag Karl Alber, pp. 85–103.

Thompson JB (2005) *Books in the digital age: The transformation of academic and higher education publishing in Britain and the United States.* Cambridge: Polity Press.

UCU (2013) The Research Excellence Framework: UCU Survey Report. www .ucu.org.uk/media/6005/The-Research-Excellence-Framework-REF–UCU-Survey-Report-Oct-13/pdf/REF-survey-report-September-2013.pdf (accessed 22 February 2021).

UKRI (2021) UKRI Open Access Policy. www.ukri.org/wp-content/uploads/2021/08/UKRI-180821-UKRIOpenAccessPolicy-2.pdf (accessed 14 October 2021).

Ullrich P (2016) Prekäre Wissensarbeit im akademischen Kapitalismus: Strukturen, Subjektivitäten und Organisierungsansätze in Mittelbau und Fachgesellschaften. *Soziologie* 45(4): 388–412. http://publikatio nen.soziologie.de/index.php/soziologie/article/view/878 (accessed 29 March 2023).

    (2019) Organisierung und Mobilisierung im akademischen Kapitalismus. *Komplexe Dynamiken globaler und lokaler Entwicklungen: Verhandlungen des 39. Kongresses der Deutschen Gesellschaft für Soziologie in Göttingen 2018.* https://depositonce.tu-berlin.de/handle/11303/10523 (accessed 22 February 2021).

van Dalen HP and Henkens K (2012) Intended and unintended consequences of a publish-or-perish culture: A worldwide survey. *Journal of the American Society for Information Science and Technology* 63(7): 1282–93. https://doi.org/10.1002/asi.22636.

van Dijk D, Manor O, and Carey LB (2014) Publication metrics and success on the academic job market. *Current Biology* 24(11): R516–17. https://doi.org/10.1016/j.cub.2014.04.039.

Vannini P (2006) Dead poets' society: Teaching, publish-or-perish, and professors' experiences of authenticity. *Symbolic Interaction* 29(2): 235–57. https://doi.org/10.1525/si.2006.29.2.235.

Vostal F (2016) *Accelerating academia: The changing structure of academic time*. London: Palgrave Macmillan.

Warnecke T (2019) So viel bekommen die Exzellenzunis. *Der Tagesspiegel*. www.tagesspiegel.de/wissen/aufstellung-des-forschungsminister iums-so-viel-bekommen-die-exzellenzunis/25104274.html.

Watermeyer R and Hedgecoe A (2016) Selling 'impact': Peer reviewer projections of what is needed and what counts in REF impact case studies. A retrospective analysis. *Journal of Education Policy* 31(5), 651–65. https://doi.org/10.1080/02680939.2016.1170885.

Weber M ([1905] 2001) *The protestant ethic and the spirit of capitalism*. London: Routledge.

([1917] 2015) *Wissenschaft als Beruf*. Stuttgart: Reclam.

([1922] 1978) Economy and society. In Roth G and Wittich C (eds) *Economy and society: An outline of interpretive sociology*. New York: University of California Press.

Weisshaar K (2017) Publish and perish? An assessment of gender gaps in promotion to tenure in academia. *Social Forces* 96(2): 529–60. https://doi.org/10.1093/sf/sox052.

Wellcome Trust (2020) *What researchers think about the culture they work in*. https://wellcome.org/reports/what-researchers-think-about-research-culture (accessed 29 March 2023).

West JD, Jacquet J, King MM, et al. (2013) The role of gender in scholarly authorship. *PLOS ONE* 8(7). https://doi.org/10.1371/journal .pone.0066212.

White J (2015) Zero-hours contracts and precarious academic work in the UK. *Academic Matters*. https://academicmatters.ca/zero-hours-con

tracts-and-precarious-academic-work-in-the-uk/ (accessed 24 June 2020).

Whitley R, Gläser J and Engwall L (2010) *Reconfiguring knowledge production: Changing authority relationships in the sciences and their consequences for intellectual innovation.* Oxford: Oxford University Press.

Williams B (2008) *Philosophy as a humanistic discipline.* Princeton, NJ: Princeton University Press.

Wissenschaftsrat (2014) Empfehlungen zu Karrierezielen und -wegen an Universitäten. *Publikationen des Wissenschaftsrats.* www.wissenschafts rat.de/download/archiv/4009-14.pdf (accessed 22 February 2021).

Wohlrabe K, Gralka S, and Bornmann L (2019) Zur Effizienz deutscher Universitäten und deren Entwicklung zwischen 2004 und 2015. *ifo Schnelldienst* 72(21): 15–21. www.ifo.de/DocDL/sd-2019-21-wohl rabe-gralka-bornmann-effizienz-universitaeten-2019-11-07_1.pdf.

Wood EM (2016) *Origin of capitalism: A longer view.* London: Verso.

Young MD (1994) *The rise of the meritocracy.* New Brunswick, NJ: Transaction.

Cambridge Elements ☰

Publishing and Book Culture

SERIES EDITOR
Samantha Rayner
University College London

Samantha Rayner is Professor of Publishing and Book Cultures at UCL. She is also Director of UCL's Centre for Publishing, co-Director of the Bloomsbury CHAPTER (Communication History, Authorship, Publishing, Textual Editing and Reading) and co-Chair of the Bookselling Research Network.

ASSOCIATE EDITOR
Leah Tether
University of Bristol

Leah Tether is Professor of Medieval Literature and Publishing at the University of Bristol. With an academic background in medieval French and English literature and a professional background in trade publishing, Leah has combined her expertise and developed an international research profile in book and publishing history from manuscript to digital.

About the Series

This series aims to fill the demand for easily accessible, quality texts available for teaching and research in the diverse and dynamic fields of Publishing and Book Culture. Rigorously researched and peer-reviewed Elements will be published under themes, or 'Gatherings'. These Elements should be the first check point for researchers or students working on that area of publishing and book trade history and practice: we hope that, situated so logically at Cambridge University Press, where academic publishing in the UK began, it will develop to create an unrivalled space where these histories and practices can be investigated and preserved.

Cambridge Elements $\equiv$

Publishing and Book Culture

Academic Publishing

Gathering Editor: Jane Winters

Jane Winters is Professor of Digital Humanities at the School of Advanced Study, University of London. She is co-convenor of the Royal Historical Society's open-access monographs series, New Historical Perspectives, and a member of the International Editorial Board of Internet Histories and the Academic Advisory Board of the Open Library of Humanities.

ELEMENTS IN THE GATHERING

A full series listing is available at: www.cambridge.org/EPBC

Printed in the United States
by Baker & Taylor Publisher Services